Results are a by-product.

Postpone gratification.

Seek joy.

Embrace generosity.

Ship the work.

Learn from what you ship.

Avoid reassurance.

Dance with fear.

Be paranoid about mediocrity.

Learn new skills.

Create change.

See the world as it is.

Get better clients.

Be the boss of the process.

Trust your *self*.

Repeat.

PORTFOLIO/PENGUIN

The
Practice

The Practice

Shipping
Creative
Work

Seth Godin

Portfolio / Penguin
An imprint of Penguin Random House LLC
penguinrandomhouse.com

Most Portfolio books are available at a discount when purchased in
quantity for sales promotions or corporate use. Special editions, which
include personalized covers, excerpts, and corporate imprints, can be created
when purchased in large quantities. For more information, please call (212)
572-2232 or email specialmarkets@penguinrandomhouse.com. Your local
bookstore can also assist with discounted bulk purchases using the Penguin
Random House corporate Business-to-Business program. For assistance in
locating a participating retailer, email B2B@penguinrandomhouse.com.

Image on page 32 courtesy of Drew Dernavich.
All other images courtesy of the author.

Library of Congress Cataloging-in-Publication Data

Names: Godin, Seth, author.
Title: The practice: shipping creative work / Seth Godin.
Description: New York: Portfolio, 2020.
Identifiers: LCCN 2020025982 (print) | LCCN 2020025983 (ebook) |
ISBN 9780593328972 (hardcover) | ISBN 9780593328989 (ebook)
Subjects: LCSH: Creative ability.
Classification: LCC BF408 .G557 2020 (print) |
LCC BF408 (ebook) | DDC 153.3/5—dc23
LC record available at https://lccn.loc.gov/2020025982
LC ebook record available at https://lccn.loc.gov/2020025983

Printed in Canada
1 3 5 7 9 10 8 6 4 2

Book design by Alexis Farabaugh

The magic of the creative process
is that there is no magic

The Practice

Shipping
Creative
Work

Seth Godin

Portfolio / Penguin
An imprint of Penguin Random House LLC
penguinrandomhouse.com

Most Portfolio books are available at a discount when purchased in
quantity for sales promotions or corporate use. Special editions, which
include personalized covers, excerpts, and corporate imprints, can be created
when purchased in large quantities. For more information, please call (212)
572-2232 or email specialmarkets@penguinrandomhouse.com. Your local
bookstore can also assist with discounted bulk purchases using the Penguin
Random House corporate Business-to-Business program. For assistance in
locating a participating retailer, email B2B@penguinrandomhouse.com.

Image on page 32 courtesy of Drew Dernavich.
All other images courtesy of the author.

Library of Congress Cataloging-in-Publication Data

Names: Godin, Seth, author.
Title: The practice: shipping creative work / Seth Godin.
Description: New York: Portfolio, 2020.
Identifiers: LCCN 2020025982 (print) | LCCN 2020025983 (ebook) |
ISBN 9780593328972 (hardcover) | ISBN 9780593328989 (ebook)
Subjects: LCSH: Creative ability.
Classification: LCC BF408 .G557 2020 (print) |
LCC BF408 (ebook) | DDC 153.3/5—dc23
LC record available at https://lccn.loc.gov/2020025982
LC ebook record available at https://lccn.loc.gov/2020025983

Printed in Canada
1   3   5   7   9   10   8   6   4   2

Book design by Alexis Farabaugh

*The magic of the creative process
is that there is no magic*

A genius is the one most like himself.

THELONIOUS MONK

Realer than real, truer than true.

STEVEN PRESSFIELD

Trust Your
Self

Shipping, because it doesn't count if you don't share it.

Creative, because you're not a cog in the system. You're a creator, a problem solver, a generous leader who is making things better by producing a new way forward.

Work, because it's not a hobby. You might not get paid for it, not today, but you approach it as a professional. The muse is not the point, excuses are avoided, and the work is why you are here.

Lost in all the noise around us is the proven truth about creativity: it's the result of desire—the desire to find a new truth, solve an old problem, or serve someone else. Creativity is a choice, it's not a bolt of lightning from somewhere else.

There's a practice available to each of us—the practice of embracing the process of creation in service of better. The practice is not the means to the output, the practice *is* the output, because the practice is all we can control.

The practice demands that we approach our process with commitment. It acknowledges that creativity is not an event, it's simply what we do, whether or not we're in the mood.

Sculptor Elizabeth King said it beautifully, "Process saves us from the poverty of our intentions."

Learn to juggle. Draw an owl. Make things better. Without regard for whether it's going to work this time. The practice will take you where you seek to go better than any other path you can follow. And while you're engaging in the practice, you'll honor your potential and the support and kindness of everyone who came before you.

1. It's Possible

This is a book for people who want to lead, to write, or to sing.

For people who seek to teach, to innovate, and to solve interesting problems.

For people who want to go on the journey to become a therapist, a painter, or a leader.

For people like us.

It's possible. The people who came before us have managed to speak up, stand up, and make a difference. While each journey is unique, each follows a pattern—and once you see it, it's yours.

We simply need to find the courage to be more creative. The forces that are holding us back have long been unseen, but we can see and understand them and begin to do our work.

The practice is there if we're willing to sign up for it. And the practice will open the door to the change you seek to make.

2. The Pattern and the Practice

Our lives follow a pattern.

For most of us, that pattern was set a long time ago. We chose to embrace a story about compliance and convenience, the search for status in a world constrained by scarcity.

The industrial economy demands it. It prods us to consumption and obedience. We trust the system and the people we work for to give us what we need, as long as we're willing to continue down the path they've set out for us. We were all brainwashed from a very early age to accept this dynamic and to be part of it.

The deal is simple: follow the steps and you'll get the outcome the system promised you. It might not be easy, but with effort, just about anyone can do it.

So we focus on the outcome, because that's how we know we followed the steps properly. The industrial system that brainwashed us demands that we focus on outcomes to prove we followed the recipe.

That priority makes sense if the reliable, predictable outcome really matters and the payoff is truly guaranteed. But what happens when your world changes?

Suddenly, you don't always get what was guaranteed. And the tasks you're asked to do just aren't as engaging as you'd like them to be. The emptiness of the bargain is now obvious: you were busy sacrificing your heart and your soul for prizes, but the prizes aren't coming as regularly as promised.

The important work, the work we really want to do, doesn't come with a recipe. It follows a different pattern.

This practice is available to us—not as a quick substitute, a recipe that's guaranteed to return results, but as a practice. It is a persistent, stepwise approach that we pursue for its own sake and not because we want anything guaranteed in return.

The recipe for recipes is straightforward: good ingredients, mise en place, attention to detail, heat, finish. You do them in order. But when we create something for the first time, it's not as linear, not easily written down.

This new practice takes leadership, a creative contribution—something that not just *anyone* can produce, something that might not work but that might be worth pursuing. It's often called "art."

The industrial system we all live in is outcome-based. It's about guaranteed productivity in exchange for soul-numbing, predirected labor. But if we choose to look for it, there's a different journey available to us. This is the path followed by those who seek change, who want to make things better.

It's a path defined by resilience and generosity. It's outward focused, but not dependent on reassurance or applause.

Creativity doesn't repeat itself; it can't. But the creative journey still follows a pattern. It's a practice of growth and connection, of service and daring. It's also a practice of selflessness and ego in an endless dance. The practice exists for writers and leaders, for teachers and painters. It's grounded in the real world, a process that takes us where we hope to go.

This practice is a journey without an external boss. Because there's no one in charge, this path requires us to trust ourselves—and more importantly, our *selves*—instead.

The Bhagavad-Gita says, "It is better to follow your own path, however imperfectly, than to follow someone else's perfectly." Consider the people who have found their voice and made a real impact: their paths always differ, but their practices overlap in many ways.

At the heart of the creative's practice is trust: the difficult journey to trust in your *self*, the often hidden self, the unique human each of us lives with.

See the pattern, find your practice, and you can begin to live the process of making magic. Your magic. The magic that we need right now.

3. Are You Searching for Something?

Most of us are.

If we care enough, we keep looking for that feeling, that impact, that ability to make a difference. And then we look harder.

Followers aren't searching. They're simply following in the footsteps of the people before them. Do well on the test, comply with the instructions, move to the next rung.

Leaders seek to make things better, to contribute and to find firm footing. The chance to make a difference and to be seen and respected, all at once.

That search has created our culture and the world we live in. More and more people, engaging and contributing, weaving together something worth building.

Let's call it *art*. The human act of doing something that might not work, something generous, something that will make a difference. The emotional act of doing personal, self-directed work to make a change that we can be proud of.

We each have more leverage than ever before. We have access to tools, a myriad of ways forward, and a real chance to contribute.

Your part matters. Your art matters.

It's worth reminding yourself that the question isn't "can I make art," because you already have.

You have already spoken up at least once, contributed something that mattered. You've said something funny to a friend or perhaps even sold out Carnegie Hall.

And now we need you to do it again. But more so.

The real question is: "Do I care enough to do it again?"

As John Gardner wrote, "The renewal of societies and organizations can go forward only if someone cares."

4. Askıda Ekmek

Askıda ekmek: there is bread on the hook. It's an ancient tradition in Turkey. When buying a loaf at the local bakery, you can choose to pay for an extra loaf and, after bagging your purchase, the owner will hang the second loaf on a hook on the wall.

If a person in need comes by, he or she can ask if there's anything on the hook. If so, the bread is shared, and the hunger is relieved. Perhaps as important, community is built.

When you choose to produce creative work, you're solving a problem. Not just for you, but for those who will encounter what you've made.

By putting yourself on the hook, you're performing a generous act. You are sharing insight and love and magic. And the more it spreads, the more it's worth to all of those who are lucky enough to experience your contribution.

Art is something we get to do for other people.

5. Finding a Practice

Do you have a creative hero? Someone who regularly leads, creates, and connects? Perhaps they're a dancer, a recording artist, or a civil rights lawyer. In every field of endeavor, some people stand out as the makers of what's next, as the voices of what's now.

Here are some to get you started: Patricia Barber, Zaha Hadid, Joel Spolsky, Sarah Jones, Yo-Yo Ma, Tom Peters, Frida Kahlo, Banksy, Ruth Bader Ginsburg, Bryan Stevenson, Liz Jackson, Simone Giertz, Jonas Salk, Muhammad Yunus, Rosanne Cash, Greta Thunberg, John Wooden, Amanda Coffman—

living or dead, famous or not, there are change-makers in every corner of our culture.

With few exceptions, the careers and working processes of every one of these artists are similar. Their output is different, the circumstances are different, and the timing is different, but the practice remains.

We can adopt a practice as well.

Maybe we don't need an industrial-strength recipe for what it means to do our jobs. Maybe instead of a series of steps to follow, we'd be better off understanding how the world actually works now.

We can adopt a practice. Here are the surprising truths that have been hidden by our desire for those perfect outcomes, the ones industrial recipes promise but never quite deliver:

- Skill is not the same as talent.

- A good process can lead to good outcomes, but it doesn't guarantee them.

- Perfectionism has nothing to do with being perfect.

- Reassurance is futile.

- Hubris is the opposite of trust.

- Attitudes are skills.

- There's no such thing as writer's block.

- Professionals produce with intent.

- Creativity is an act of leadership.

- Leaders are imposters.

- All criticism is not the same.

- We become creative when we ship the work.

- Good taste is a skill.

- Passion is a choice.

Throughout this book, we'll keep returning to surprising truths like these that fly in the face of what we've been taught about productive work in a system based on compliance and recipes. Artists have been shunned or shamed for embracing them, but that's because these truths work. They subvert the dominant power structure while at the same time they enable us to make things better for the people we seek to serve.

6. Learning to Juggle

I've taught hundreds of people how to juggle. Learning requires a simple insight: catching the ball isn't the point.

People who fail to learn to juggle always fail because they're lunging to catch the next ball. But once you lunge for a ball, you're out of position for the next throw, and then the whole thing falls apart.

Instead, we begin with just one ball. And there's no catching: throw/drop, throw/drop, throw/drop. Twenty times we throw the ball from our left hands, watching it land each time.

And then we do it again with our right hands.

Practicing how to throw. Getting good at throwing. If you get good enough at throwing, the catching takes care of itself.

It turns out that all this dropping is the hardest part for someone who is learning to juggle. It makes them really uncomfortable to throw a ball and then stand there as it drops to the ground. The desire for outcome is deeply ingrained, and for some, this is the moment where they give up. They simply can't bear a process that willingly ignores the outcome.

For those who persist, the process quickly gathers momentum.

Perhaps fifteen minutes later, we try throw/throw/drop/drop. Simply two balls and two throws.

And then, without stress, throw/throw/catch/catch. It's easy. There's no problem, because the throws are where they should be, rehearsed and consistent.

The process has gotten us this far.

And then the last step is to add a third ball.

It doesn't always work, but it always works better than any other approach.

Our work is about throwing. The catching can take care of itself.

7. How to Draw an Owl

It's a classic meme, based on an old comic book instruction manual.

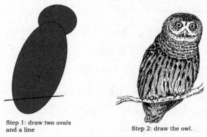

How to draw
an owl.

Step 1: draw two ovals
and a line

Step 2: draw the owl.

The humor lies in all the steps that are missing. Everyone knows how to draw two ovals and a line. No one, least of all me, knows how to draw the owl.

It highlights our desire to run from the pain of not being sure. The headline promises instruction, as life does. But, just like life, the headline is lying to us.

For the important work, the instructions are always insufficient. For the work we'd like to do, the reward comes from the fact that there is no guarantee, that the path isn't well lit, that we cannot possibly be sure it's going to work.

It's about throwing, not catching. Starting, not finishing. Improving, not being perfect.

No one learns to ride a bike from a manual. And no one learns to draw an owl that way either.

8. Does It Take Courage to Be Creative?

We care enough to stand as a leader, whether on the stage or behind the keyboard, and say, "Here, I made this." For some, this moment of being judged—where we're nothing but an imposter acting as if we belong—is overwhelming.

And so, too often, we walk away from a creative life, a chance to be generous, an opportunity to solve problems. Or, if we pursue it, we do it gingerly, treating creativity as a fragile magic trick, the gift of the muse. If we must be creative, we try to do it out of the corner of our eye. Staring at the magic directly is frightening.

Nonsense.

It doesn't have to be this way. We don't have to wait to be picked and we don't have to stand by, hoping that we will feel our calling. And we certainly don't have to believe in magic to create magic.

Instead, we can model the process of the successful creatives who have come before us. We can go on a journey with our eyes wide open, trusting the process and ourselves to create our best contribution.

This is our chance to make things better.

Being creative is a choice and creativity is contagious.

9. This Is Art

Not painting, but art: the act of doing something that might not work, simply because it's a generous thing to do. The combination of talent, skill, craft, and point of view that brings new light to old problems. The way we change our culture and ourselves.

Painting is something you do to a house. Art is the work we do where there is no right answer—and yet the journey is worth the effort. We might make art with a keyboard, with a paintbrush, or with our actions. Mostly, we do it because we lean into a practice, trusting we have a shot at making a difference.

We do it without a guarantee, with simply a practice we've chosen to commit to.

Are you an artist? Of course you are.

Artists make change happen. Artists are humans who do generous work that might not work. Artists aren't limited to paint or museums.

You're an artist as soon as you announce you are. As a leader, a coach, a contributor, a designer, a musician, an impresario . . . it's art if you let it be. If you care enough.

Legendary designer and illustrator Milton Glaser said, "One of the problems with art is that it is self-anointing: Anyone can be an artist by simply pointing to themselves and saying so. The truth is that there are very few artists. [Making the world a better place through art] is the highest attainment of the specialization. It is to recognize that it is not all about you, and that you have a communal function you can serve to help everyone get along. This is important for people to understand, especially in a capitalist society."

You can choose to find your voice, or you can continue to ignore it.

10. Perhaps You Can Make Some Art

Art is what we call it when we're able to create something new that changes someone.

No change, no art.

When we ship our best work (at least our best in this moment), we have a chance to turn it into art. And then we have a chance to do it again.

It's a form of leadership, not management. A process without regard for today's outcome, a commitment to the journey.

You were born ready to make art. But you've been brainwashed into believing that you can't trust yourself enough to do so.

You've been told you don't have enough talent (but that's okay, because you can learn the skill instead).

You've been told you're not entitled to speak up (but now you can see how many others have taken their turns).

And you've been told that if you can't win, you shouldn't even try (but now you see that the journey is the entire point).

Art is the generous act of making things better by doing something that might not work.

11. Creativity Is an Action, Not a Feeling

Marie Schacht points out that we can't always do much about how we feel, particularly when it's about something important. But we can always control our actions.

Your work is too important to be left to how you feel today.

On the other hand, committing to an action can change how we feel. If we act as though we trust the process and do the work, then the feelings will follow.

Waiting for a feeling is a luxury we don't have time for.

12. The Story (and the Choice)

I have a story in my head, all about how things are supposed to be. You might have one, too. And that story drives the actions that we take.

Often, we'll go to ridiculous lengths to make the story come true. The story might be one of entitlement or talent. It might be one of injustice or privilege. Often, though, the story is based on lowered expectations, the seduction of compliance, and the avoidance of failure.

We keep trying to make the existing narrative true, because that's a lot more comfortable than the alternative.

"Here we go again" is an easy way to lull yourself into victimhood, a place where the work is no longer up to you.

If we believe that it's not our turn, that we're not talented enough, we'll do whatever we can to make that story true. We'll sit back and wait to be chosen instead.

That's backward.

Most of the time, the story we live by came from somewhere. It might be the way we were raised, or it could be the outcome of a series of events. Burn yourself on the stove and you might persuade yourself that you should go nowhere near a stove. Grow up in a home with low expectations and it's possible you'll begin to believe them. The story we tell ourselves leads to the actions we take.

If you want to change your story, change your actions first. When we choose to act a certain way, our mind can't help but rework our narrative to make those actions become coherent.

We become what we do.

13. Flow Is a Symptom

We've all experienced it, and once we do, we itch to do it again.

That moment when distractions fade away, when the narrative backs off and the chatter dies down, when we're directly engaged with the work.

It might happen on a long hike or in a brainstorming session. It often happens when we're making art that matters.

But for many of us, it appears too rarely.

That might be because we're waiting for it to arrive. We're expecting it to choose us. We think the conditions have to be exactly right, since any deviance from them will cause it to evaporate.

But what if we built flow into the process? What if it were a choice?

Some creators use a blank piece of paper as a trigger. Others feel that way at the piano keyboard or when they take the podium at a meeting.

If we condition ourselves to work without flow, it's more likely to arrive.

It all comes back to trusting our *self* to create the change we seek. We don't agree to do that after flow arrives. We do the work, whether we feel like it or not, and then, without warning, flow can arise.

Flow is a symptom of the work we're doing, not the cause of it.

14. It's Time to Find Your Voice

You can find the way forward, a path toward making a difference.

There is a method, but it has no fixed steps.

There is a strategy, but the tactics don't really matter.

There is a process, but it doesn't always work.

The practice that is open to us always works better than anything else we could try.

Take the time to see what's worked before. Watch the creative heroes around us who have raised their hands, taken the lead, and created something that matters. Again and again, the work falls into a pattern, often containing counterintuitive twists and turns.

You can start where you are.

You can see and you can be seen.

You can listen and you can be heard.

And you can do the work that you were born to do.

Sometimes, we opt for more instead of better.

But better is better than more.

15. Finding Your Passion

One question comes up in my podcast (at akimbo.link) the most often: where do I find my passion? And the corollary: if I'm not passionate about my work, what should I do?

Once you decide to trust your *self*, you will have found your passion. You're not born with it, and you don't have just one passion. It's not domain-specific: it's a choice.

Our passion is simply the work we've trusted ourselves to do.

This is worth deconstructing, because the strategy of "seeking your calling" gives you a marvelous place to hide.

After all, who wants to do difficult work that doesn't fulfill us? Who wants to commit to a journey before we know it's what we were meant to do?

The trap is this: only after we do the difficult work does it become our calling. Only after we trust the process does it become our passion.

"Do what you love" is for amateurs.

"Love what you do" is the mantra for professionals.

16. The Process and the Outcome

We live in an outcome-focused culture. A plumber doesn't get credit for effort; he gets credit if the faucet stops leaking. A corporation is rarely judged on the long-term impact of how it treats its employees; it is judged on its earnings per share.

A short-term focus on outcomes means that we decide if a book is good by its bestseller rank, if a singer is good based on winning a TV talent show, and if a child athlete is good based on whether or not she won a trophy.

Lost in this obsession with outcome is the truth that outcomes are the results of process. Good processes, repeated over time, lead to good outcomes more often than lazy processes do.

Focusing solely on outcomes forces us to make choices that are banal, short-term, or selfish. It takes our focus away from the journey and encourages us to give up too early.

The practice of choosing creativity persists. It's a commitment to a process, not simply the next outcome on the list. We do this work for a reason, but if we triangulate the work we do and focus only on the immediate outcome, our practice will fall apart.

Our commitment to the process is the only alternative to the lottery-mindset of hoping for the good luck of getting picked by the universe.

Forgive the repetition, but it's here for a reason. A lifetime of brainwashing has taught us that work is about measurable results, that failure is fatal, and that we should be sure that the recipe is proven before we begin.

And so we bury our dreams.

We allow others to live in our head, reminding us that we are impostors with no hope of making an original contribution.

Our practice begins with the imperative that we embrace a different pattern, a pattern that offers no guarantees, requiring us to find a process and to trust ourselves.

As Susan Kare, designer of the original Mac interface, said, "You can't really decide to paint a masterpiece. You just have to think hard, work hard, and try to make a painting that you care about. Then, if you're lucky, your work will find an audience for whom it's meaningful."

It might not be what we want to hear, but it's true.

17. The World's Worst Boss

You might work for the world's worst boss.

The boss might be a jerk.

The boss might not recognize all the good work that you do.

The boss might do a lousy job of lining up better clients to keep you busy.

Or might not reward you for all the insight and care and passion you bring to the job.

In fact, the boss might bother you at home in the middle of the night for no good reason. Waking you up so that you can worry a little bit more about work. And mostly the boss might have the wrong expectation of what you're capable of creating.

You've probably guessed who I'm talking about.

The world's worst boss might very well be you.

Because the most important boss whom each of us answers to is ourselves. And what it means to have a better boss is to have a boss who raises the bar for us but still gives us a break when we fail. What we need is a boss who is diligent and patient and insightful.

We need a boss who trusts us.

Sometimes I use the phrase "trust your self," with three words instead of two. Who is "your"? Who's doing the trusting and who's being trusted?

What we need is a boss who can trust us enough to look ahead with confidence as we go on this journey.

Someone who can line up the next gig before it's an emergency. Someone who doesn't panic, doesn't seek external validation at every turn. And someone who is in it for the long haul.

Most of all, what we need from a great boss, for our *self*, is somebody who will see us for what we are capable of.

You would never work for somebody who treats you the way that you treat your *self*.

It's time to start training the boss that is you. Time to start trusting your *self*, trusting the process, and trusting that you are actually as capable as you are.

18. You Are Enough

The industrial system works to make you feel powerless. Its message is that you haven't been chosen, haven't been given the right talents, and aren't worthy of having a voice.

But you are already enough.

You already have enough leverage.

You already see enough.

You already want to make things better.

Start where you are. Start now. Find the pattern and care enough to do something about it.

19. An Aside about Decisions

Annie Duke, former world champion of poker, teaches us that there's a huge gap between a good decision and a good outcome. A good decision is based on what we know of the options and the odds. A good outcome happens or it doesn't: it is a consequence of the odds, not the hidden answer.

Just as a good process doesn't guarantee the outcome you were hoping for, a good decision is separate from what happens next.

Flying across the country is safer than driving. If your goal is to get to Reno, the safest choice is to fly there, not to drive.

And if you know of someone who dies in a plane crash on the way to Reno, they didn't make a bad decision when they chose to fly. There was certainly a bad outcome, though.

Decisions are good even if the outcomes aren't.

The same is true for the process of generous creativity. The process is a smart one even if the particular work doesn't resonate, even if the art doesn't sell, even if you are aren't happy with the reaction from the critics.

That's because what we seek and how we create aren't the same thing.

Reassurance is futile—and focusing on outcomes at the expense of process is a shortcut that will destroy your work.

20. To Be of Service

Isn't that what we're here to do?

To do work we're proud of.

To put ourselves on the hook.

To find the contribution we're capable of.

The only way to be on this journey is to begin.

But there isn't a guarantee. In fact, most of what we seek to do will not work. But our intent—the intent of being of service, of making things better, of building something that matters—is an essential part of the pattern.

Because most of us, most of the time, act without intent.

21. The Work and the Guarantee

The practice has nothing at all to do with being sure the work is going to be successful. That's a trap.

The guarantee requires industrial sameness, recipes that have been tested, and most of all, the fungible labor of the disrespected laborer. If anyone can do it, then we'll just hire anyone.

Doing the work simply involves acknowledging that we're capable of caring enough to make the work better. To learn, to see, and to improve.

The search for a guarantee is endless, fruitless, and the end of possibility, not the beginning.

In perhaps the most profound remark I can recall hearing from a member of Black Sabbath, drummer Bill Ward said this about their first hit: "I thought the song would be a flop, but I also thought it was brilliant."

22. I Feel Like an Imposter

At least when I'm doing my best work.

The imposter syndrome had been around long before the term was coined in 1978 by Pauline Clance and Suzanne Imes. It's that noise in our heads that reminds us we have no business raising our hand, jumping in the water, or standing on stage.

And I feel like an imposter often.

That's because my best work involves doing things I've never done before.

Recent research estimates that 40 percent of the workforce has a job that requires innovation, human interaction, and decision making. And for each of these people, every day exposes them to the feeling of being a fraud.

Of course you're not sure it's going to work. How could you be?

The person you're serving might take offense, or walk away, or simply might not speak the same language.

Of course there's no manual, no proven best practices, no established rulebook. The very nature of innovation is to act as if—to act as if you're on to something, as if it's going to work, as if you have a right to be here. Along the way, you can discover what doesn't work on your way to finding out what does.

23. Imposter Syndrome Is Real

It's a sign that you're healthy and that you're doing important work. It means that you're trusting the process and doing it with generosity.

Confidence isn't the same as trust in the process. Confidence is a feeling we get when we imagine that we have control over the outcome. When Joe Namath guaranteed that he would lead the Jets to the Super Bowl, he was sharing his confidence with the media.

Every pro athlete is confident, but more than half of them lose. Every game, every tournament, has confident entrants who don't win. Requiring control over external events is a recipe for heartache and frustration. Worse, if you need a guarantee you're going to win before you begin, you'll never start.

The alternative is to trust the process, to do our work with generosity and intent, and to accept every outcome, the good ones as well as the bad.

Yes, you're an imposter. But you're an imposter acting in service of generosity, seeking to make things better.

When we embrace imposter syndrome instead of working to make it disappear, we choose the productive way forward. The imposter is proof that we're innovating, leading, and creating.

24. Start Where You Are

Identity fuels action, and action creates habits, and habits are part of a practice, and a practice is the single best way to get to where you seek to go.

Before you are a "bestselling author," you're an author, and authors write. Before you are an "acclaimed entrepreneur," you're simply someone who is building something.

"I am ———— but they just don't realize it yet" is totally different from "I'm not ———— because they didn't tell me I was."

The only choice we have is to begin. And the only place to begin is where we are.

Simply begin.

But begin.

Imogen Roy helps us understand that effective goals aren't based on the end result: they are commitments to the process. That commitment is completely under your control, even if the end result can't be.

But the only way to have a commitment is to begin.

25. Who You Are (and What You Do)

We are easily confused by "I am."

"I am six feet tall," isn't a choice. It's a given.

On the other hand, "I am a chef," is up to you (or not).

We've been fooled into believing that roles like "writer," "leader," and "artist" are birthrights, fixed in place, something we either are or we aren't. That leaders are given talents or privileges, not choices.

The truth is simpler: If you want to be a leader, then lead. If you want to be a writer, then write.

"I am of service" is something each of us can choose to become. It only takes a moment to begin.

And once you begin, you are.

The discomfort and skepticism you might feel when you encounter the simplicity of this reshuffling (do *then* be) is precisely why we need to embrace a practice. It's not easy or comfortable to switch from a lifetime of compliance and convenience to work with a new rhythm, a new set of principles, and a new way of being in the world. That discomfort is a good sign. It means that you're beginning to see the pattern.

26. How Big Is the Discard Pile?

Drew Dernavich is at the top of his field. He has published more classic cartoons in *The New Yorker* than just about anyone else.

What a dream job. Sit at home in your pajamas, be funny for a few minutes, draw a sketch, and get paid for it.

Apparently, this is not only fun to do, but it's reserved for a true talent, a genius, someone who has figured it out.

That's why the internet erupted when Drew published this picture of his desk:

Drew's not a genius. He just has more paper than us.

How many cartoons would you need to have rejected before you gave up?

On the other hand, how many not-very-good cartoons would you have to draw before you figured out how to make them funny?

These might be related.

27. Dave Grohl's Mom

Rock and Roll Hall of Fame drummer Dave Grohl said, "Dr. Dre, Michael Stipe, Zac Brown, Pharrell . . . people like that, you'd think that there wouldn't be like any sort of common parallel because everybody is so different. But all of their stories are almost exactly the same. In this window of ten to thirteen years' old, all of these kids decided they wanted to become musicians."

His mom wrote a book about it.

She explained that she, and so many of the other moms, saw this desire in their kids and decided to let it flourish.

It's not important that the kids developed their musical skills when they were eleven. It's important that they developed the habit of identity. When they looked in the mirror, they saw themselves as musicians, as artists, as people who had committed to a journey.

There's nothing magic about being eleven years old. Except that it's easier to develop an identity when you don't have to walk away from one you've already developed.

The practice doesn't care *when* you decide to become an artist. What simply matters is that you decide. Whether or not your mom is involved in the decision.

28. Toward a Daily Practice in Service of Your Identity

Julia Cameron's morning pages help unlock something inside. Not the muse or a magic mystical power, but simply the truth of your chosen identity. If you do something creative each day, you're now a creative person. Not a blocked person, not a striving person, not an untalented person. A creative person.

Because creative people create.

Do the work, become the artist. Instead of planning, simply become. Acting as if is how we acquire identity.

Writing is a universal solvent for creatives. Painters, entrepreneurs, therapists, circus acts—each of us can write our story down, a permanent record of how we see the world and how we will change the world.

Yes, you can do it in private, in a notebook that no one will ever see. But you will find so much more juice if you do it in public. Even if you use an assumed name. Even if you only circulate it to a few people.

Knowing that the words are there, in front of others, confirms your identity.

"I wrote this."

Blog every day. It's easy, it's free, and it establishes your identity long before the market cares about who you are and what you do.

Writers write. Runners run. Establish your identity by doing your work.

29. "So Far" and "Not Yet"

You haven't reached your goals (so far).

You're not as good at your skill as you want to be (not yet).

You are struggling to find the courage to create (so far).

This is fabulous news. It's been going on since you were a kid. Something isn't there when you want it (or need it) but then it is. Persistent and consistent effort over time can yield results.

"So far" and "not yet" are the foundation of every successful journey.

30. In Defense of Magic

Close-up magic, mentalism, and even the grand stage illusions of a magician in a top hat are effective for a very simple reason: we don't know the trick.

The tension of seeing something happen that we know to be impossible, combined with our confidence that the impossible couldn't have happened—that's why magic acts work. And the urge to know how it's done is natural but must be resisted, because once we know how it's done, all the tension (and with it our interest, and the magic) instantly disappears.

The same is true of our appreciation of art. We'd like to believe that we're communing with the universe, that the muse has whispered a reserved truth to the creative who brought us the work. We'd like to believe that showing up to play jazz is fundamentally different than showing up to work at the Department of Motor Vehicles.

It might be easier to experience awe if we believe the person who created the work also experienced the same thing.

I'm a sucker for writing about the creative process. I love imagining what it would feel like to stare deep into the void, to be touched by His Noodly Appendage, to feel the heavens dictating to me as I move to a transcendent state.

Except . . .

Except that's not how the trick is done.

The trick isn't a trick at all. It's a practice that begins with trusting yourself to show up and do the work.

31. Trust, Identity, and Your Practice

Trust is not self-confidence.

Trust is a commitment to the practice, a decision to lead and make change happen, regardless of the bumps in the road, because you know that engaging in the practice is better than hiding from it.

There are people and organizations in our lives that we trust. How did that happen? We develop trust over time. Our interactions lead to expectations, and those expectations, repeated and supported, turn into trust.

These organizations and people earn trust by coming through in the difficult moments. They're not perfect; in fact, the way they deal with imperfection is precisely why we trust them.

We can do the same thing to (and with) ourselves. As we engage in the practice, we begin to trust the practice. Not that it will produce the desired outcome each time, but simply that it's our best available option.

Trust earns you patience, because once you trust yourself, you can stick with a practice that most people can't handle.

And the practice is available to all of us.

32. Fly-Fishing Lessons

My friends Alan and Bill ran a small event in Wyoming, and on the third day, they woke us all up at 5:00 a.m. so we could go take a fly-fishing lesson

I'd always wanted to experience the sport, but I had no desire to actually catch a fish, even if I was going to release it later. So, when the instructor set me up with my rod, I asked him for a fly without a hook. He gave me an odd look, but he found one in his kit.

The next few hours were extraordinary, not least because I knew that there was no way I was going to catch a fish.

My friends were busy trying to catch something. You could see it in all of their actions—they were willing, hoping, and imploring the fish to somehow bite the hook.

Relieved of this easily measured outcome, I could focus on the practice alone. I focused on the rhythm, on my posture, on the magic of the physics of casting.

At some point, the professional has to bring home the fish. That's the fuel that permits the professional to show up each day. But the catch is the side effect of the practice itself. Get the practice right, and your commitment will open the door for the market to engage with your work.

When Elizabeth King said, "Process saves us from the poverty of our intentions," she was talking about the fish. You might seek a shortcut, a hustle, a way to somehow cajole that fish onto the hook. But if it distracts you from the process, your art will suffer. Better to set aside judging yourself until after you've committed to the practice and done the work.

33. The Poverty of Our Intentions

In any given moment, the world isn't perfect.

Conditions aren't right. The economy hits a bump. There's a

health emergency. Our confidence is shaken. A particularly nasty comment gets through our filter. We're rejected.

The list is long indeed.

And in those moments, our intentions might not be pure. We might want to hide, or seek the muse. We might want to sell out or settle or simply give up.

But the practice saves us.

Because the practice can be trusted.

And because in this moment it's simply the best next step.

34. The Practice Is Relentless

The Danyang–Kunshan Grand Bridge is the longest railroad bridge in the world, at an astonishing 102 miles long. That's more than half a million feet in length.

On the other hand, the Bosideng Bridge is also the longest bridge in the world, but it's only 1,700 feet long. About 1/500th the length.

What's the difference?

The Bosideng Bridge is the longest single-span bridge in the world. The water's too deep for there to be any supports, so it has to cross the river in one giant leap.

On the other hand, the Danyang–Kunshan is thousands of spans long. It's not a single bridge at all, it's a series of bridges.

The career of every successful creative is part of a similar practice: a pattern of small bridges, each just scary enough to dissuade most people.

The practice requires a commitment to a series of steps, not a miracle.

Generous

35. You Have the Right to Remain Silent

But I hope you won't.

The world conspires to hold us back, but it can't do that without our permission.

The dominant industrial system misrepresents the practice, pretending that it's about talent and magic. The system would prefer you to stand by, quietly. It says, "Please sign up for the status-driven recipe of insufficiency, compliance, and applause."

We don't need more noise, more variety, or more pitches. There's noise all around us, but it's often the idle chatter of people hiding in plain sight, or the selfish hustle of one more person who wants something from you. Our world is long on noise and short on meaningful connections and positive leadership.

Your contribution—the one that you want to make, the one you were born to make—that's what we're waiting for, that's what we need.

36. The Generous Vision

Selling can feel selfish. We want to avoid hustling people, and so it's easy to hold back in fear of manipulating someone. Here's an easy test for manipulation: if the people you're interacting with discover what you already know, will they be glad that they did what you asked them to?

Artists have a chance to make things better by making better things. Contributing work to those whom they serve. Turning on lights, opening doors, and helping us not only connect to our better nature, but to one another.

Industrialists seek to make what's requested, and to do it ever cheaper and faster. But people who have found their voice are able to help us see that life includes more than what's requested.

You're not a short-order cook. You're here to lead us.

37. What Do You Sound Like when You Sound Like You?

One way to avoid criticism (and to distrust our own voices) is to sound like everyone else. When we mimic talking points or work hard to echo what the others have said, we're hiding. We're doing it with the support of the system, the one that would prefer we be a commodity, an easily replaceable cog in the factory.

Everyone has a voice in their head, and every one of those

voices is different. Our experiences and dreams and fears are unique, and we shape the discourse by allowing those ideas to be shared. It might not work. But only you have your distinct voice, and hoarding it is toxic.

Of course you're allowed to sound like you. Everyone else is taken.

38. Hoarding Is Toxic

Hoarding your voice is based on the false assumption that you need to conserve your insight and generosity or else you'll run out of these qualities. Hoarding is a way to hide from the fear of being insufficient. Hoarding isolates you from the people who count on you and need you the most.

If you don't think you'll have a good idea ever again, you'll hesitate to share what you do have, because you're worried that it will be stolen and you'll be left with nothing.

A scarcity mindset simply creates more scarcity, because you're isolating yourself from the circle of people who can cheer you on and challenge you to produce more. Instead, we can adopt a mindset of abundance. We can choose to realize that creativity is contagious—if you and I are exchanging our best work, our best work gets better. Abundance multiplies. Scarcity subtracts. A vibrant culture creates more than it takes.

If we don't trust our voice, or if we haven't found it yet, it's easy to justify our silence. Better, we think, to hold back than to be rejected.

Our failure to trust ourselves can consume us. The scarcity cycle turns us selfish and makes us fail to trust others as well.

Art lives in culture and culture exists because we're actively engaging with each other.

39. Twenty Cents and a Soccer Ball

Kennedy Odede grew up in abject poverty in Kibera, a slum in Kenya. In 2004, with nothing to invest but time and passion, he started SHOFCO, a nonprofit designed to help youth in Kibera.

He began by organizing a soccer team, then continued to grow an organization focused on generosity. They now offer medical clinics, clean water, public toilets, and other free services throughout several poor regions in Kenya. Not because there was a series of assignments or a job to be filled, but because they could.

Kennedy grew up surrounded by insufficiency. It's a feeling many of us have been taught to feel. It's so easy to decide to focus on ego—*our* urgencies, *our* agenda, *our* needs. But he made a different choice, the choice to focus externally and generously instead.

If you lived in a village where the water was riddled with disease, and you figured out how to purify the water, would you share the idea for free with the other villagers?

Selfishly, you might wonder if that's fair. After all, you did all the work. And you might never have another idea as good as this one.

In practice, though, a village with clean water is going to be a lot more productive. That productivity is going to raise the standard of living for everyone, producing more food, more well-being, and more joy for everyone. No matter the financial return, that joy will come back to you many times over.

Our culture is like that village. Ideas shared are ideas that spread, and ideas that spread change the world.

40. Pythagoras and the Fifth Hammer

Pythagoras, the guy who invented the hypotenuse, led a cult of brilliant but sometimes confused mathematicians. They believed that harmonics held the key to understanding how things functioned. At the heart of their work was the study of ratios, of dividing things into their basic components in search of the secret of the universe.

According to myth, Pythagoras was stuck on a theory, so he went for a walk to clear his head. He passed a blacksmith's shop and heard five workers inside, all using hammers to bend iron. As their hammers struck in rhythm, the clang organized into a beautiful sound, with all the hammers singing out in beautiful harmony at once.

He walked into the blacksmith's shop and, with a bluster that would have been fun to watch, took all five hammers away with him.

He wanted to study what made their harmony so haunting . . . it might unlock the secret he was seeking.

Over the following weeks, Pythagoras weighed and measured each hammer. He wanted to understand why they didn't make identical sounds and, more importantly, why they sounded so good when they all clanged at the same time.

His work helped us discover a physical connection between math and the world. It turns out that the ratios in the weights of the first four hammers led to their ringing in harmony—each had a weight that was a multiple of the other. More fascinating to me, though, is that the fifth hammer didn't follow any of the rules of harmony. The fifth hammer was spurious, data that didn't fit, something to be ignored.

Like many researchers throughout time, Pythagoras threw out the fifth hammer (and the pesky mismatch) and published his work only about the first four. But it turns out that the misfit, the fifth hammer, was the secret to the entire sound. It worked precisely because it wasn't perfect, precisely because it added grit and resonance to a system that would have been flaccid without it.

The harmonies of Crosby, Stills, Nash, and Young often worked best because of Neil Young—because his voice didn't fit.

Young was the fifth hammer.

During CSNY's breakout tour in 1974, the core trio traveled

together, often by private jet, from gig to gig. Young refused to fly with them, instead leaving immediately after each concert and driving to the next gig in an old mobile home, accompanied only by his son. He was their friction, the wild card, the fifth hammer.

The fifth hammer is the one that's not proven, not obvious, or not always encouraged.

The fifth hammer is you, when you choose the practice and trust yourself enough to create.

41. When Was the Last Time You Did Something for the First Time?

Nostalgia for a future that hasn't happened yet is a modern affliction. We spend our days imagining that tomorrow might not be what we're hoping for, filled with regret about what might have been. We see what's possible, we know that we have a chance to make things better—and yet we hesitate.

That better future seems to drift away, becoming evanescent as we find ourselves looking away with regret. It's not only when there's a worldwide pandemic. Every day, it seems that doors are closing, that the perfect tomorrow we hoped for isn't going to arrive.

There's nothing that we can do to ensure that tomorrow turns out exactly as we hope it will. It might be easier to turn away from possibility and simply let the winds buffet us, a victim of whatever is happening around us.

The alternative is to find a foundation to stand tall. We can choose to take our chance, to speak up, and to contribute.

42. Sailing with the Wind at Your Back

The easiest way to go through life is to let life go through you. Give in to the prevailing winds and go along to get along. This requires very little effort because you're not working with intent— at least not your own intent. You're getting by. Doing your best. Perhaps even just doing your job.

But of all the usable directions, a sailboat goes *slowest* when it is going downwind. That's because the sail acts as a parachute, meaning the boat can't go any faster than the wind behind it. Dandelions spread their seeds at the whims of the wind, but they don't make much of an impact.

The sailboat doesn't work that way. The sailboat is optimized to go *across* the wind. The fastest sailboat direction is beam or close reach, heading perpendicular or even toward the wind.

We can do this with our work. We can find a direction and a craft. We can trust a process to enable us to get better and better at the work we do.

We make a difference in the world when we seek to make a difference.

Not because it's easy, but because it matters.

This is all part of the practice.

43. The Hospitality of Discomfort

My colleague Marie Schacht differentiates between hospitality (welcoming people, seeing them, understanding what they need) and comfort (which involves reassurance, soft edges, and an elimination of tension).

But art doesn't seek to create comfort. It creates change. And change requires tension.

The same is true for learning. True learning (as opposed to education) is a voluntary experience that requires tension and discomfort (the persistent feeling of incompetence as we get better at a skill).

The practice, then, is to not only cause temporary discomfort for those whom you lead, serve, and teach, but to embrace your own discomfort as you venture into territories unknown. Artists actively work to create a sense of discomfort in their audience. Discomfort engages people, keeps them on their toes, makes them curious. Discomfort is the feeling we all get just before change happens. But this new form of hospitality—of helping people change by taking them somewhere new—can make us personally uncomfortable as well. It might feel easier to simply ask people what they want and do that instead.

Choosing to offer only comfort undermines the work of the artist and the leader. Ultimately, it creates less impact and less hospitality as well.

Your discomfort is no excuse for being inhospitable. Our practice is to bring a practical empathy to the work, to realize that in our journey to create change, we're also creating discomfort.

For our audience. And for ourselves.

And that's okay.

44. Diversity and Problem Solving

Problems have solutions. That's what makes them problems. A problem without a solution isn't a problem, it's simply a situation.

Solvable problems are usually solved by surprising, non-trivial alternatives. If an obvious solution from an obvious source could have provided an answer, it would have happened already.

Instead, it's the unlikely approaches—the odd combinations that come from diversity—that often win the day.

Diversity might involve ethnicity or physical abilities. But it's just as likely to involve idiosyncratic approaches and differences in experience. If enough peculiar people get together, something new is going to happen. Author Scott Page has shown that as systems get more complex, diversity creates ever more benefits.

Of course, each of us is peculiar in our own way. Peculiar is a choice, an opportunity to bring our own experiences and our own point of view to the work. We've been trained for a long time to hide that unique voice or to pretend it's not there, because the systems around us push us to conform. So much so that the word "peculiar" has taken on a shameful cast for some—when it simply means *specific*.

But in a world that's changing faster than ever, that distinct skill set and point of view are precisely what we need from you.

Without your specific contributions, our diversity of approach and experience fades away.

45. Bradley Cooper Has a Cold

You're the executive producer on a big new Netflix series, and it turns out that your star won't be able to make the beginning of the shoot. It's about a crusading lawyer and a single parent, and it's a juicy role. You're in a jam and you need a replacement.

The studio gives you a day to solve the problem. They need someone who has been nominated for Academy Awards, perhaps won a Golden Globe, and has done more than four billion dollars at the box office.

Quick, make a list. Who are the five or six stars you might go after?

When faced with this challenge, most people don't suggest Scarlett Johansson, Don Cheadle, or Gwyneth Paltrow, even though all three are among the ten people who might fit the requirements.

That's because these choices don't match our instinct to avoid specifics and peculiarities. We're pushed to default to the "regular kind" even if that's not going to solve our problem. Even if it's unfair.

The same instinct to match whatever narrative is dominant pushes us to fit in instead of to stand out. It amplifies our fear at the same time it diminishes our contribution.

46. "Here, I Made This"

"I" as in me, you, us, the person who's on the hook. This is the work of a human. The audience can make a direct connection between you and the thing you're offering.

"Made" because it took effort, originality, and skill.

"This" is not a wishy-washy concept. It's concrete and finite. It didn't used to exist, and now it does. This is peculiar, not generic.

"Here," because the idea is a gift, a connection transferred from person to person.

These four words carry with them generosity, intent, risk, and intimacy.

The more we say them, and mean them, and deliver on them, the more art and connection we create.

And we create change for a living.

47. Change-Makers in Charge

It's pretty simple, this new reality:

You're here to make change. We need to make things better, and we need someone to lead us.

Time is fleeting and you only get today once.

Now that you're in charge, there are three simple ways you can make that change with more focus, energy, and success.

First, you can embrace the fact that you can, in fact, trust the process and repeat the practice often enough to get unstuck.

Second, you can focus on the few, not everyone.

And third, you can bring intention to your work, making every step along the way count.

You may not be on the well-trodden path, but wherever you're headed, it's important.

48. No Place to Hide

Hiding is pleasant. If it weren't for the way it leads to suffering a thousand small deaths, hiding would be a comfortable way to coast through life.

But if we trust ourselves and seek to make change happen, hiding can no longer be an option.

Stand-up comedy is the most naked of the mass entertainments. One person, one microphone, no costumes. You can't blame the script or the lighting or the band. It's simply you, sharing a story.

When you bomb, there's no place to hide. That's part of the attraction for the comic. The tightrope is high and it hurts when you fall.

There are other ways to make an impact than enduring the grueling grind of stand-up, of course. Each of them requires finding a way to not hide. To say, "Here, I made this." To trust yourself enough to ship the work.

Of course, it might not work. That's built into the process. Do it anyway.

And then do it again.

If you care enough, it's worth doing as many times as it takes.

49. The Best Reason to Say "No"

Writer Justine Musk reminds us that in order to say no with consistency and generosity, we need to have something to say "yes" to. Our commitment to the practice is the source of that yes.

The world expects that its requests will be accepted. That assignments, lunch dates, new projects, and even favors will get a yes. It's just a small ask, the person thinks.

The problem is obvious—if you spend all day hitting the ball back, you'll never end up serving.

Responding or reacting to incoming asks becomes the narration of your days, instead of the generous work of making your own contribution.

Should you check your email or work on your book?

Deciding to answer the email counts as a yes. But it might be a yes to the wrong thing.

It might be that the most generous thing to do is to disappoint someone in the short run.

Inbox zero is a virtuous habit, though an exhausting one. Like all forms of responsiveness, it favors the short term over the long, the urgent over the important. And it comes with a juicy deniability, a way to spend an hour or two without having to own too much.

That inbox might be your email, or it might be the way you control your calendar, plan your next project, or deal with your sister-in-law. There's always a list of things that others would like from you, and we spend far more time than we realize sorting and fulfilling this list.

I rarely answer an email while giving a speech or when I'm deep in the middle of a new workshop or idea. Because in those moments, I've committed to what writer Derek Sivers calls the "hell yeah."

Generous doesn't always mean saying yes to the urgent or failing to prioritize. Generous means choosing to focus on the change we seek to make.

It's difficult to find what author Rosalyn Dischiavo calls "the deep yes." This sort of selective prioritization requires responsibility and vulnerability. And it requires process. The people-pleasing power of an indiscriminate yes is a form of resisting the yes of shipping our real work. It cuts us off from the connection that we desperately seek.

When you own your agenda, you own it. That means you're responsible, without excuses about why you might be hiding or explanations about why you're busy.

It's easy for a self-focus to turn selfish. Saying no too often is a recipe for solipsism, a form of egomania that is just as selfish as the one we were trying to walk away from. Out of balance, a self-trusting no at all costs becomes yet another way to hide.

If your no becomes a habit, a way to hide out, you may end up cutting ties with the very people you set out to serve. And if your no becomes too seductive, you can get comfortable there instead, never actually shipping your work, because shipping your work means that you'll need to reenter the world with a yes. We commit to making people uncomfortable in the short run so we can be hospitable later.

If you're results-focused, if the trust you had in your *self* has become a fragile cycle in need of reassurance, shipping your work to the world is fraught. And so it might be easier to stay warm in the narcissism of always saying yes. Or always saying no.

But that surrender means you've sacrificed the most generous (and frightening) thing you can do: trusting yourself enough to show up and ship the work. The right work to the right people for the right reason.

50. Reassurance Is Futile

Very few three-word mantras are more disturbing than "reassurance is futile." But once you embrace the practice, you'll realize that it's true.

"Everything is going to work" isn't true. It can't be.

We reassure kids because they don't have enough experience and they don't know what to expect. And we reassure kids because we're pretty sure that we can protect them.

But seeking reassurance isn't helpful when we work to make change happen. Because doing something that might not work means exactly that . . . that it might not work.

While it's calming to be reassured, it never lasts. As soon as we hear the words, the feeling begins to fade away. There's never enough reassurance to make up for a lack of commitment to the practice. We have no choice other than to trust ourselves enough to lead the way.

Reassurance is simply a short-term effort to feel good about the likely outcome. Reassurance amplifies attachment. It shifts our focus from how we persistently and generously pursue the practice to how we maneuver to make sure that we're successful. We focus on the fish, not the casting.

Reassurance is helpful for people who seek out certainty, but successful artists realize that certainty isn't required. In fact, the quest for certainty undermines everything we set out to create.

Hope is not the same as reassurance. Hope is trusting yourself to have a shot to make things better. But we can hope without reassurance. We can hope at the same time that we accept that what we're working on right now might not work.

51. The Fear of Falling Behind

Kiasu is the Hokkien word for "the fear of being left behind" or not getting enough. It's a common affliction, not only in Singapore, where the phrase originates, but around the world. Far more than FOMO, it's a grasping insufficiency that drives many people forward.

We've amplified a feeling of scarcity to encourage people to comply. To get them to buy more stuff (before it's all gone), to work ever harder (because someone is going to overtake you), and to live in fear. It leads to panic buying and hoarding. And it's an effective way to motivate students when you're seeking compliance, or to manipulate a crowd into pushing itself.

Of course, *kiasu* is actually about fear and insufficiency. And it couldn't exist if we trusted ourselves enough to know that we're already on a path to where we seek to go.

If you are using outcomes that are out of your control as fuel

62

for your work, it's inevitable that you will burn out. Because it's not fuel you can replenish, and it's not fuel that burns without a residue.

52. Confidence Is Relative

An inch is always an inch long. It's an absolute, easy to measure. That's why we use it.

It's tempting to want our feelings to be absolute: provable and fungible and tangible. But confidence varies from person to person and from day to day. Confidence is a feeling, and feelings are difficult to measure and control. Reassurance is futile because it seeks to shore up a feeling, and in any given moment, it might or might not do the job.

We don't have to be victim to our feelings. They don't have to arrive or leave of their own accord. We can choose to take actions that will generate the feelings we need.

Glenn Close has been nominated for seven Academy Awards. She's never won. If she were focused on winning an Oscar for performance, she never would have created the body of work that she did. Is she a failure? Was her acting career a waste? Does the lack of peer reassurance say anything at all about her body of work? If she were measuring her practice based on a vote that is out of her control, she'd be basing her decisions on incorrect data.

The practice is a choice. With discipline, it's something we can *always* choose. The practice is there for us, whether or not we feel confident.

Especially when we don't feel confident.

53. Resistance Is Real

Steven Pressfield's masterful *The War of Art* taught us to see the force he calls resistance. Resistance is an elusive and wily force, an emotion that will conspire to block us, undermine us, or, at the very least, stall us in the pursuit of work that matters.

Resistance focuses obsessively on bad outcomes because it wants to distract us from the work at hand. Resistance seeks reassurance for the same reason.

Resistance relentlessly pushes us to seek confidence, then undermines that confidence as a way to stop us from moving forward.

But if we don't need confidence, if we can merely trust the practice and engage in the process of creation and shipping, then resistance loses much of its power.

Generosity is the most direct way to find the practice. Generosity subverts resistance by focusing the work on someone else. Generosity means that we don't have to seek reassurance for the self, but can instead concentrate on serving others. It activates a different part of our brain and gives us a more meaningful way forward. People don't want to be selfish, and giving in to resistance when you're doing generous work feels selfish.

Our work exists to change the recipient for the better. That's at the core of the practice.

When you're doing the work for someone else, to make things better, suddenly, the work isn't about you. Jump in the water, save that kid.

54. Consider the Locksmith

You're locked out of your home. You call a locksmith for help. He comes over and begins to try master keys on your lock.

Each key is tried, one by one. There's a process. The stakes for the locksmith are low. He knows he has a finite number of keys. He knows that it's likely that one will fit. If one doesn't fit, he knows he can go back to the office and get another set.

As each key is tried, there's no emotion involved. He's not viewing this as a referendum on his abilities as a locksmith. He's just seeking to help. Besides, trying each key is a moment for feedback. Does this key fit this lock? Data is being collected. Ultimately, he'll find a key that fits (or he won't).

The professional locksmith doesn't match our vision of the working artist. But what about the professional software engineer? She writes a line of code, compiles it, sees if it works. A bug isn't personal. It's another bit of data. Adjust the code and repeat.

Or perhaps it's worth considering the therapist. He tries one way to engage with a recalcitrant patient. It succeeds or it fails. He does it on their behalf. And then another, and another, until the process yields a result.

And the same is true for the playwright. She brings a few pages of dialogue to a workshop and has the actors engage with it. It might work for some in the audience but not others. Does it land with the right people? Again, it's not fraught, because the risks were understood when the process began. Now is not the time for reassurance: it's the time for useful feedback.

For art to be generous it must change the recipient. If it doesn't, it's not working (yet). But realizing it's not working is an opportunity to make it better.

The practice is agnostic about the outcome. The practice remains, regardless of the outcome.

55. The Generosity of the Pennies

Annie Dillard had a quirky habit at the age of seven. She would hide a shiny penny in the crook of a tree, then put signs in chalk on the road, directing people passing by to find her hidden treasure.

"There are lots of things to see, unwrapped gifts and free surprises. The world is fairly studded and strewn with pennies cast broadside from a generous hand. But—and this is the point— who gets excited by a mere penny?"

The penny is dramatically underrated. Most everyone gets excited by being noticed, connected, or truly seen. The essence of your art isn't that it comes from a rare place of genius. The magic is that you chose to share it.

Writer Dan Shipper worked on his first book when he was seven, too. His hack for producing a book in third grade was to fill it with one character reciting an endless series of numbers. The other part of his hack was somehow persuading his grandfather to type it.

Everyone involved in the project remembered it for the rest of their lives.

You can produce more than you know if you are intent on doing it for someone else.

56. Embracing (Yet)

I slipped in a parenthetical earlier: "It's not working (yet)."

That's the only reassurance you truly need.

There's a practice. The practice is proven, and you've embraced it.

Now, all that's needed is *more*.

More time, more cycles, more bravery, more process. More of you. Much more of you. More idiosyncrasy, more genre, more seeing, more generosity. More learning.

It's not working. (Yet.)

57. Cynicism Is a Defense Mechanism

And not a particularly effective one.

Positive people are more likely to enjoy the practice. They're not wasting any time experiencing failure in advance.

Negative artists engage in the practice as well, but they suffer more.

It's tempting to prepare yourself against inevitable failure. Perhaps by becoming a pessimist and a cynic, you could spread your suffering out over time. If your expectations are low, you won't be disappointed.

Too often, though, that suffering becomes a self-fulfilling prophecy, a habit we hold on to that infects our work. Pessimists might try to insulate themselves from disappointment, but they're probably preventing themselves from shipping important work instead. If generosity is at the heart of our practice, how does cynicism help us become more generous?

If we can model being positive about our practice, the outcome will take care of itself.

It's worth noting that I used the word "failure" above, but that's not really what we're talking about. If you ship generous work and it doesn't connect with the desired audience, you may have had an outcome you didn't hope for, but the practice itself isn't a failure.

Of my 7,500 blog posts, half of them are below average compared to the others, on any metric you'd care to measure. Popularity, impact, virality, longevity. That's simple arithmetic.

The practice embraces that simple truth.

It's all a way of understanding that if you have a practice, failure (in quotes if you wish) is part of it.

No need to gird yourself for it with cynicism. You could, if you chose, celebrate the opportunity instead.

58. Practical Empathy

People don't know what you know, don't believe what you believe, and don't want what you want.

And that's okay.

It's impossible to be appropriately generous to everyone. Because everyone is different.

We have to be able to say "it's not for you" and mean it.

The work exists to serve someone, to change someone, to make something better. In order to be popular, to reach the masses, we often have to sacrifice the very change we sought to make.

Change *someone*. And, as Hugh MacLeod said, "Ignore everyone."

In *This Is Marketing*, I wrote about practical empathy. This is the posture of the successful creator.

Having empathy might make you a good person, but it also makes you a better creative.

It's not helpful to only make things for yourself, unless you're fortunate enough that what you want is precisely what your audience wants.

You don't need to be a toddler to design toys, or a cancer survivor to be an oncologist. Part of the work involves leaving the safety of our own perfectly correct narrative and intentionally entering someone else's.

And so, there's the challenge of embracing the gulf between what you see or want or believe and what those you're serving see, want, or believe. Because they're never the same. And the only way to engage with this gap is to go where they are, because those you serve are unlikely to care enough to come to you.

59. "Someone" Saved TV

Network television was the greatest mass-market success story in history. From 1960 to 1990, more people watched the same thing at the same time than ever before (and probably ever again). With only three major networks in the United States, it wasn't unusual for a TV show to have 30 million simultaneous viewers.

The result of trying to attract everyone was *Gilligan's Island*. And *Three's Company*.

The golden age of TV didn't arrive until HBO and other cable networks started creating shows like *The Sopranos* and *Mad Men*.

But it's worth noting that a typical episode of *Mad Men* was only seen by 3 or 4 million people when it aired.

It would have been canceled immediately if it had been on network TV a decade earlier.

It took programmers and creators who were seeking someone, not everyone, to give us TV we could be proud of. TV we now take for granted.

Yes, the most popular shows on Netflix are shows that evolved into crowd-pleasers like *The Office*. But you don't create a hit by trying to please everyone.

60. Shun the Nonbelievers

A key component of practical empathy is a commitment to not be empathic to everyone.

A contemporary painter must ignore the criticism or disdain that comes from someone who's hoping for a classical still life. The tech innovator has to be okay with leaving behind the laggard who's still using a VCR. That's okay, because the work isn't for them.

"It's not for you" is the unspoken possible companion to "Here, I made this."

There's nothing wrong with the non-believers. They don't have a personality disorder and they're not stupid. They're simply not interested in going where you're going, not educated in the genre in which you work, or perhaps not aware of what your core audience sees.

If we can't embrace this, and if our focus is on external validation, then the journey will always be fraught. It's culturally impossible to do important work that will be loved by everyone. The very act of being "important" means that it will have a different impact on people. The alternatives are:

1. You can choose to make work that's banal. Work that's so indifferent or mediocre that no one bothers to dislike it (which also means that it's unlikely that people will love it). This is incredibly common, the source of almost all wasted creative work.

2. You can choose to create work only for yourself, ignoring genre, the market, and any feedback. Every once in a while, a breakthrough arrives through solipsism. But it's hard to imagine anyone who collaborates with others being able to productively work in this way.

That leaves the option of trusting your *self*. This combines two choices:

1. Choose to make work that matters a great deal to *someone*. Develop an understanding of genre, work to see your

audience's dreams and hopes, and go as far out on the edge as they're willing to follow. Choose to be peculiar.

2. Choose to commit to the journey, not to any particular engagement. Because you're dancing on a frontier, it's impossible that all of your work will resonate. That's okay. Great work isn't popular work; it's simply work that was worth doing.

If you're on a journey but it's rarely causing a spark, you probably need to make better work. Braver work. Work with more empathy. Once you learn to see, you can learn to improve your craft. Combined with your commitment to the practice, it's inevitable you'll produce an impact. If you care enough.

61. But Maybe It Needs More Work

If there are only non-believers, the reason is simple: you're not seeing genre the way others do.

In other words, it's not as good as you think it is—if you define "good" as work that is resonating with the people you seek to serve.

That's part of the practice. To embrace the fact that the audience isn't wrong, you're just not right (yet).

It's worth pausing for a moment to see the fork in the road again. It's honorable for your art to be just for you. For you to choose to create for an audience of one. But that's not professional work, because you're not on the hook. There's no one to serve but you and the idea in your head.

The other route is to become a working professional, a leader, someone who chooses to ship creative work. And shipping means that it's for someone.

To commit to that path is a brave and generous act. And it puts you on the hook to see the audience clearly enough, and to be brave enough, to develop the empathy needed to create generous work.

62. And Maybe You're Trying to Do Two Things at Once

The first thing is making exactly what you want, for you.

And the second thing is making something for those you seek to connect and change.

Pursuing *either* is fine. Pursuing *both* is a recipe for unhappiness, because what you're actually doing is insisting that other people want what you want and see what you see.

Most of us would like that—we might even deserve it after all the work we invest—but that doesn't mean it's likely to happen.

63. Three Thousand Sold

General Magic invented the future. And then it went out of business.

Megan Smith, Andy Hertzfeld, Marc Porat, and the rest spent the 1990s inventing virtually every element of the modern smartphone. The form factor, the interface, the partnerships . . .

And their first model sold exactly three thousand units.

They were ten years ahead of their time. The business failed, but the project didn't.

Their failure was in setting expectations for a mass audience. They built an organization that promised to change the world overnight and brought their ideas to the wrong audience (of investors, of media, of users) in a way that they couldn't sustain.

The project changed the world. As William Gibson has said, "The future is already here—it's just not very evenly distributed." Every cultural change follows precisely the same uneven path.

64. Three Kinds of Quality

English is a surprisingly nonspecific language, and the multiple meanings of common words often trips up our ability to understand what's being discussed. "Quality" is one of those words.

On a Saturday night in February, in the heart of New York,

two Broadway musicals were performed just a few blocks from each other.

One was the groundbreaking and legendary *Hamilton*. It contained all three sorts of quality.

The other was the new revival of *West Side Story*. It only had two.

The technical meaning of quality comes from pioneering consultants Edwards Deming and Phil Crosby. This is the quality of car manufacture. In short, quality means meeting spec.

A 1995 Toyota Corolla was a better-quality car than a 1995 Rolls Royce Silver Shadow. That's because the Toyota had better-quality parts, parts that met strict tolerances. The Toyota didn't rattle or ping, and it was far less likely to need repairs.

In the theater, this sort of quality means that the actors don't forget their lines and the lighting is to spec. In the case of *West Side Story*, it means that the video screens they used were the brightest, highest-resolution screens most people have ever seen.

On the other hand, the more vernacular understanding of quality means luxury. Most people would say a Rolls Royce is better quality than a Toyota, but that simply describes its elite status, the cost of the materials used, the luxe-ness of it all.

A Broadway show definitely meets this definition of quality. At $900 a ticket, it's a lot more rare and more expensive than taking your date to a movie.

But the third definition of quality is the one that's relevant here. And this is the quality of creative magic.

Despite the huge budget that director Ivo van Hove lavished on his *West Side Story*, it is missing the creative magic that is so evident, even years later, when you walk down the street to see *Hamilton*.

In *West Side Story*, everyone remembers their lines. It rains buckets in the final scene with Maria and Tony, perfectly executed. It's polished and shiny and expensive.

But the quality of art can't compare.

If you have a choice of just one of the three qualities, it's the last one that matters.

65. Four Kinds of Good

"This is what I saw in my head." (It's good to me.)

"This is accepted and admired by a specific circle of people." (It's good for the tribe.)

"I got paid well for this." (I'm clear about what matters to me.)

"This is really popular, it's a hit." (We struck a chord with the masses.)

The kind you might hope for but can't get is: every single critic likes it.

The first kind of good, the good of seeing what you wanted to see when you began to create, is essential but insufficient for the professional. If the work is your hobby, if you're doing it only for yourself, this is all you need. But for anyone who seeks to make an impact and change the culture, we need more.

Being accepted and admired by your specific audience is another sort of good—and for most of us, this is actually enough. I believe this is the goal of a working creative. This is the secure spot in the circle of those who matter to you. This is the ability to continue to do your work for people who care. This is where we can produce without feeding the beast of "more."

The successful cartoonist for *The New Yorker* is in this group, as is the Burning Man performance artist or the jazz musician who regularly sells out the Blue Note. Almost all truly great work lives in this sort of good.

Chasing the third kind of good requires us to spend time worrying about becoming a hack. Simply getting paid a lot for your TV pilot or the startup you sold to a giant company doesn't mean that the work itself is what you set out to do. On the other hand, in a world where almost everything is given a value in dollars and cents, getting paid well for your work might be proof that you've achieved your goal.

And the last type of good, the one that distracts so many who engage in the process, is the feeling that comes from creating a monster hit. A piece of work that crosses over from the core audience to a much larger one. This is the bestseller list or the line out the door. This is the TED talk with forty million views.

Chasing this elusive sort of perfection is a challenging task, because the numbers are stacked against you (many entries, few winners). It also puts a lot of focus on outcomes, instead of on the practice.

That means that because most of the time you won't go viral, it's worth producing work you're proud of, even if you don't have a hit in the end.

66. The Confusion: Is a Hit Good?

My friend J. runs one of the most successful music labels in the world. He's had a ton of No. 1 hits. I asked him what the hardest part of creating a hit record was. Without hesitation, he replied, "Finding good songs."

"What," I asked, "makes a good song?"

Straight-faced, he said, "It becomes a hit."

Bob Lefsetz, the music journalist, recently wrote about "Dance Monkey," a song by the Australian act Tones and I. The song was a hit in dozens of countries, just not in the U.S. His post was met with dozens of responses, most from music industry leaders. A&R professionals, label heads, and producers all chimed in with their take on the music Tones and I created.

You can probably guess what they said. Half of the letters said that Toni, the force behind the music, was incredibly talented and a future great. The other half denigrated her song and her work, largely because it hadn't been a hit in their community.

There's a significant gap between what the market buys and what some consider worth engaging with. It's easy to get confused by hits, but a hit might not be your goal.

67. Selling Is Difficult

Amateurs often feel like they're taking something from the prospect—their time, their attention, and ultimately, their money. That, after all, is what car dealers taught us to experience.

Even if you get paid for it, sales can feel like harrowing work. Small-scale theft, all day every day.

But what if you recast your profession as a chance to actually solve someone's problem? A doctor who prescribes insulin to a diabetic isn't selling insulin; she's generously saving a life.

The car dealer who steers you away from a lemon and into a car that will serve your family well is creating value for you.

And the songwriter who works hard to get a song on the radio—one that you haven't heard before—is doing the generous work of creating a new hit, a hit that becomes part of your history and cultural vocabulary.

Selling is simply a dance with possibility and empathy. It requires you to see the audience you've chosen to serve, then to bring them what they need. They might not realize it yet, but once you engage with them, either you'll learn what's not working in your craft or they'll learn that you've created something that they've been waiting for, something that is filled with magic.

68. Selling Is Where the Juice Lies

Is there any profession that more people seek to avoid? Even salespeople work hard to avoid making sales calls.

It's hard to imagine a bookkeeper who spends his day not keeping books, or a doctor who actively avoids seeing her patients.

But sales . . .

It's not surprising that true sales (as opposed to order-taking, which is a different thing entirely) is anathema to many people.

Sales is about change: turning "I never heard of it" into "no" and then "yes."

Sales is about upending the status quo of what the world was like before you got there. Not for you, not for your selfish reasons, but for the people who will benefit from the change you created.

Most of all, sales is about intentionally creating tension: the tension of "maybe," the tension of "this might not work," the tension of "what will I tell my boss . . ."

Why would anyone sign up to create tension?

But that's precisely the tension that we dance with as creators.

This is how we get sold on the thing we're creating before we share it. We must sell ourselves on it first, before we can sell it to anyone else.

This is why so many people have trouble with the idea of trusting themselves. Because they're bad at selling themselves on the commitment to the process.

But learning to sell to other people is the single best way to learn to sell yourself on the work, on your journey to producing something good or even better than good.

The juiciness lies in the objections, in seeing the gears turn, in hearing someone persuade themselves that they love what's on offer.

Ultimately, a successful sales call results in enrollment.

69. Enrollment

Enrollment is acknowledgment that we're on a journey together.

The Tin Man enrolls with Dorothy to go to see the Wizard. He has his own agenda. He's after his own reward, as are the Scarecrow and the Lion.

But even though each member of the troupe has their own goal in mind, they are all enrolled in the same journey, with the same agreed-upon roles and rules and, probably, time frames.

Once people are enrolled, you can get down to it. Once they're enrolled, you can play your music, paint your painting, lead your company . . .

Before that, you're spending all your time getting butts in seats, reassuring the masses, primping up the benefits of your offer.

After enrollment, though, the shift goes from "you" to "we." *We* are off to see the Wizard. *We* are engaged in this process, this journey, this performance.

To the enrolled, all we need to do is point. We can gesture over there and the team will follow. They know what it's for.

To the unenrolled, though, all we can say is "Sorry, it's not for you."

70. It's Not for You

Waiting for Godot might be my favorite play. Beckett was the Marcel Duchamp of theater, and this play is his masterpiece. Most people hate it.

They hate it because it's not where they want to go for two hours in a theater. They hate it because it's not the journey they signed up for. They hate it because it doesn't remind them of the kind of plays they actually like.

Does that mean that Beckett shouldn't have written the play, or does it simply mean that the play isn't for everyone?

Being hated by many (and loved by a few) is a sign that the work is idiosyncratic, worth seeking out, and worth talking about.

(One of the reasons that the Beckett play is so disliked is that it doesn't have a result. It is, ironically for our purposes, completely about process. The tension of possible resolution is never concluded.)

In 1956, when the play debuted on Broadway, it competed against *The Ponder Heart*, *The Reluctant Debutante*, *The Sleeping Prince*, *Time Limit!*, *Too Late the Phalarope*, *Troilus and Cressida*, *Uncle Willie*; and *Wake Up, Darling*, among others. Every one of those plays was enthusiastically promoted by someone who thought they'd be a crowd-pleaser.

Our desire to please the masses interferes with our need to make something that matters. The masses want mass entertainment, normal experiences, and the pleasure of easy group dynamics. The masses want what the masses want. We already have plenty of stuff that pleases the masses.

And of course, a few generations later, when all of the other plays of its time are likely forgotten, the one that few understood persists.

The practice demands that we seek to make an impact on someone, not on everyone.

71. Selfish Is a Choice

There will always be people who live in the shadows, who hit and run, who take as much as they can get away with.

But those acts aren't an essential part of showing up in the world, any more than the few people who cheat in a marathon are indicative of everyone who enters.

My assertion is that if you're not able to trust your *self*, the pressure is on to take what you can get. *Kiasu*. Grasping.

If the only measure of your worth is in the outcome of a transaction, not in the practice to which you've committed, then of course it makes sense to cut corners and to hustle.

We're not born to be selfish. And the economics of living in community make it clear that short-term hustle rarely benefits anyone. But when you're flailing and looking for something (anything) to stand on, there's pressure to choose the selfish path.

To a drowning man, everyone else is a stepping-stone to safety.

72. Attachment to the Outcome

What's the weather like in Vancouver today? You probably don't know or care. How deep is the powder in Telluride? Same thing.

Then, something comes along that you do care about. How will the weather be for the picnic you're planning on Saturday? If it rains, will your day be ruined?

We can spend a lot of psychic energy willing the weather to be perfect. We can spend just as much time living out the bad weather in advance, suffering ahead of time, knowing that the outcome we seek isn't going to happen the way we want it to. We want it to work out so badly, we now *need* it to.

It's easy to see the absurdity of attachment when we're talking about the weather. The thoughtful alternative is resilience. To be okay no matter how the weather turns out, because the weather happens without regard for what we need.

But what happens when we substitute the market acceptance of our new project for the weather? Or perhaps what the boss or the critics will think? When we get really attached to how others will react to our work, we stop focusing on our work and begin to focus on controlling the outcome instead.

73. Attachment Is a Choice

Attachment to the outcome. Attachment to what a certain person is going to say about our next piece of work. Attachment to our perception of our standing in the community.

We are in free fall. Always. Attachment pushes us to grab ahold of something.

Attachment is about seeking a place to hide in a world that offers us little solace.

But of course, the bad news is that there is no foundation.

We're always falling. The good news is that there's nothing to hold onto.

As soon as we stop looking for something to grab, our attention is freed up to go back to the practice, to go back to the work.

The strongest foundation we can find is the realization that there isn't a foundation.

The process of engaging with our genre, our audience, and the change we seek to make is enough. Where we stand is under our control. The practice is something we can return to whenever we choose.

Becoming unattached doesn't eliminate our foundation. It gives us one.

74. The Simple Flip to "for"

When we do work for other people, make art for other people, create opportunities for other people . . . it's natural that we should dive right into it. That's what it means to care. We're good people and doing it for someone else is a way to express our compassion.

I was in a small town, on my way to visit a friend. I stopped into a card store and asked, "Do you know if there's a florist in town?" (This was a long time ago, before I could have asked Yelp.) The shopkeeper said, "No, I have no idea where a florist might be."

There was a florist a block away.

My hunch is that the shopkeeper was tired. Tired of tourists, tired of not making a sale. And so he acted out. He probably hoped that without flowers, I'd buy some cards.

Of course, *with* flowers, I would have bought a card. But his selfish, brusque response earned him nothing much.

When we do the work *for* the audience, we open the door to giving up our attachment to how the audience will receive the work. That's up to them. Our job is to be generous, as generous as we know how to be, with our work.

Here's a simple clue: How often do you recommend a competitor? Authors blurb books for one another because they don't seek to corner the market and they understand that a mindset of abundance fuels their work. Authors and other working creatives embrace the idea that not everything they offer is for everyone. The ability to eagerly suggest an alternative to your work is a sign that your posture is one of generosity, not grasping.

75. The Two Obligations

The first obligation, as the blogger Rohan Rajiv helps us understand, is the obligation we have to the community. Once we trust ourselves to be more than invisible cogs (and perhaps even before we do that), we incur a debt. We owe the people who fed us, taught us, connected us, believed in us. We owe the people who expect something from us.

But that obligation doesn't come with a reflexive matching obligation on their part. *No one owes us anything.* Or, if they do, it's in our interest to act as if they don't.

Believing that we're owed something is a form of attachment. It's a foundation for us to count on, a chip on our shoulder for us to embrace whenever we feel afraid.

No one owes us applause or thanks. No one owes us money either.

If we choose to do work for generous reasons, and not for reciprocity or a long con but simply because we can, we stop believing that we are owed by others.

The feeling of being owed will destroy our ability to do generous work. If the audience delivers a standing ovation because they're supposed to, it's hardly worth listening to or remembering.

That's because working in anticipation of what we'll get in return takes us out of the world of self-trust and back into the never-ending search for reassurance and the perfect outcome. We believe that we need a guarantee, and that the only way to get that guarantee is with external feedback and results. It draws our eye to the mirror instead of the work.

Gratitude isn't a problem. But believing we're owed gratitude is a trap.

The feeling of being owed (whether it's true or not) is toxic. Our practice demands we reject it.

76. The Generosity of Art

The creativity you put into your work is an opportunity for better.

It opens doors and turns on lights. It connects the disconnected and creates the bonds of culture. Art transforms the recipient, even as it allows individuals to become "us."

Art is the human act of doing something that might not work and causing change to happen.

Work that matters. For people who care.

Not for applause, not for money. But because we can.

Art solves a problem for anyone who touches our work. This is the generous act of turning on a light. Not only does the light help you read, it helps everyone else in the room as well.

The thing is, shipping your art is for the audience. You've already seen it, understood it, and experienced it. But that's insufficient because without sharing the work, you can't make change happen. It's not enough to please yourself.

The rest of our process is about understanding how to become more generous. How to make more art, better art, art that's courageous.

We do this by understanding how our systems function, how our audience thinks, and how we got here. We do this by improving our craft and committing even further to our process.

77. Asking "Why" Is Brave

Asking why teaches you to see how things got to be the way they are. Asking why also puts us on the hook—it means that we're also open to being asked why, and it means that at some level, we're now responsible for doing something about the status quo.

The professional can answer your questions about why. That's one of the symptoms of being a professional. Once we embrace the process of our craft, the iterative cycle of shipping, feedback, and improvement leaves behind a vivid awareness of all the whys that came before.

And *why* compounds interest—each *why* can be followed by another, until you reach the foundational first principles of the work.

Why are the covers of hardcover books laid out like this?

Why do concerts last two hours?

Why do we need an office for our new company?

Why don't classical audiences like new music?

Asking why, even if the asking and the answers make you uncomfortable, forces you to truly look at something. And that's not only brave, it's generous.

78. If You Knew You Were Sure to Fail, Then What Would You Do?

There's no need to know the details of the practice before we begin. We can't know the recipe because there isn't a recipe: recipes are always outcome dependent.

The specific outcome is not the primary driver of our practice. If we obsess about the outcome, we're back to looking for an industrial recipe, not a way to create art.

The more important the project we take on, the more difficult it is to find certainty that our work will succeed before we begin.

We can begin with this: *If we failed, would it be worth the journey?* Do you trust yourself enough to commit to engaging with a project regardless of the chances of success?

The first step is to separate the process from the outcome.

Not because we don't care about the outcome. But because we do.

79. A Punk's Practice

A hundred years ago, Elsa von Freytag-Loringhoven, the original punk artist, and also a baroness, created a work of art that caused a sensation.

She bought a ceramic urinal at an industrial supply house and her friend Marcel Duchamp entered it into an art exhibit.

"Fountain" changed the world of art forever. It represented a shift in art, from handmade to machine-made, from pre-photography to post. In some ways, it was the end of fine art as a craft.

Duchamp, over the years, took more and more credit for the baroness's work until her name was largely forgotten. But she continued to make a ruckus. She painted, pioneered performance art, and lived a life committed to her practice.

Duchamp's theft is unforgivable, but it's Freytag-Loringhoven's passion and consistency that are noteworthy here.

She made a choice to live a life in art, to explore the penumbra, the spots just outside of the existing wisdom.

80. Choose to Go There

Your practice is a journey, and it takes you to a room. A room with different rules, different expectations, different challenges.

You know when you're in that room. You've probably been there before. Salto mortale, the dangerous leap, that feeling in your stomach when you're in thin air, neither here nor there.

Some people avoid this feeling. That's why they need a recipe and want reassurance that the work they do will pay off.

The practice requires you to seek out this experience of uncertainty, to place yourself in the room where you will create discomfort.

The
Professional

81. The Lifeguard Who Wasn't Sure

Sure, there had been the Water Safety Instructor test, and even the Bronze Medallion up in Canada, but this was still the first summer on the Michigan beach for most of the lifeguard crew. Each guard, deep down, knew that it wouldn't be difficult to find a stronger swimmer and a braver soul.

Robin Kiefer was only six that day, but already a precocious swimmer. The water was warm, so Robin slipped away from a family gathering and started to play in the waves.

But when he started to flounder in the water and go down for the second time, there wasn't any doubt about what to do. The lifeguard had learned her lessons well: uncertain or not, less qualified or not, you leap. Leap first, do your job.

Of course she wasn't sure. How could she be?

The lifeguard didn't jump in the water because she was a perfect swimmer or because she was certain that she was qualified to rescue this kid. She jumped in the water because it was her job. Because she was the closest available lifeguard. Because she had promised she would.

By the time Robin's parents got to the beach, the lifeguard had already rescued him. They never got her name, but decades later, no one has forgotten what she did.

The irony runs pretty deep. Half a century before, Robin's grandfather Adolph broke the world record in the backstroke, and the company that bears his name has sold more lifeguard buoys than any other company. And Robin is alive to tell the story because a lifeguard who wasn't certain saved a kid who needed saving.

How can any of us be certain?

And yet, how can anyone who cares hold back?

82. Yes, You're the Lifeguard

Ethicist Peter Singer asks us to consider: if you were on your way to work, wearing brand-new beautiful leather shoes, and you passed a small child, face down in a stream, would you run into the shallow water and save her life?

Of course you would.

It doesn't matter what happens to your shoes; it doesn't matter who the kid is. You can do it and so you must do it.

And the same is true, if perhaps less dramatic, when it comes to your work.

Any idea withheld is an idea taken away. It's selfish to hold back when there's a chance you have something to offer.

83. Worrying

If the problem can be solved, why worry? And if the problem can't be solved, then worrying will do you no good.

SHANTIDEVA

Worrying is the quest for a guarantee, all so we can find the confidence to press on. It's an endless search for a promise: the outcome will be worth the effort we put into the process.

Worrying is impossible without attachment. No one worries about the weather on Saturn, because no one is counting on the weather to be a certain way.

The time we spend worrying is actually time we're spending trying to control something that is out of our control.

Time invested in something that is within our control is called work. That's where our most productive focus lies.

Worrying isn't productive because it doesn't produce confidence, and even if it did, the confidence wouldn't last. Worrying is a way to hide from the fact that we are wavering on our practice.

Reassurance is futile.

The reason is simple: we need an infinite amount of reassurance, delivered daily, to build up our confidence. There will never be enough. Instead of seeking reassurance and buttressing it with worry, we could make the choice to go back to work instead.

84. Bicycle Problems

I'm having trouble learning to ride a bike.

How long have you practiced?

About fifteen minutes.

It might take a lot longer than that. It might take months.

I want to learn to ride a bike, but I don't want to fall, even once.

Not even once?

I need to be able to ride a bike blindfolded.

Have you ever seen anyone do that?

No, but that's what my inner muse is telling me I'm supposed to do.

Oh.

I want to win a bike race on a unicycle.

You can't.

Don't tell me that this person is the only one who can find a huge audience for this particular sort of bike-riding trick.

They might be.

But that's my authentic bike-riding mission. To win prizes by defeating all comers on a unicycle.

There's no promise that the world cares about your mission.

85. On the Hook or Off

The traditional way to encourage people to contribute is to let them off the hook. Look for signs of genius. Point to the mysterious muse. Encourage people to sit quietly and let that other voice take over.

I have a hundred examples. Here's one from Nobel winner Bob Dylan: "It's like a ghost is writing a song like that. It gives you the song and it goes away, it goes away. You don't know what it means. Except the ghost picked me to write the song."* This is nonsense. There is no ghost. Dylan is either fooling us or fooling himself.

In the many conversations I've had with successful creatives, it sometimes gets a bit uncomfortable. Sometimes they wonder if looking directly at their source of inspiration will make it disappear.

The source is simple: It's the self. It's us when we get out of our way. It's us when we put our *self* on the hook. No ghost. You. Us.

The industrial system has trained us to avoid the hook. Being on the hook means that you can get blamed, and getting blamed means you can get fired for what you did (or didn't do).

For some of us, though, on the hook is the best place to be. It's on you. It's on me. Our choice, our turn, our responsibility.

---

*Robert Hilburn, "Rock's Enigmatic Poet Opens a Long-Private Door," *Los Angeles Times*, www.latimes.com/archives/la-xpm-2004-apr-04-ca-dylan04 -story.html.

This is our practice.

The missing element, for so many, is our lack of trust. We feel that we somehow can't trust ourselves enough to take this on, because it's too fraught, too difficult, too risky . . .

Everything that matters is something we've chosen to do.

Everything that matters is a skill and an attitude.

Everything that matters is something we can learn.

The practice is choice plus skill plus attitude. We can learn it and we can do it again.

We don't ship the work because we're creative. We're creative because we ship the work.

No ghost is needed.

86. Talent Is Not the Same as Skill

Who are you to make a change? How dare any of us stand up and announce that we'd like to make things better.

That sort of work is for other people. People who are talented. We're told again and again that talent is a secret and rare resource that enables some to lead while others must be docile and accept what's on offer.

But that's confused.

Talent is something we're born with: it's in our DNA, a magical alignment of gifts.

But *skill*? Skill is earned. It's learned and practiced and hard-won.

It's insulting to call a professional talented. She's skilled, first and foremost. Many people have talent, but only a few care enough to show up fully, to earn their skill. Skill is rarer than talent. Skill is earned. Skill is available to anyone who cares enough.

If you put the effort into your practice, you will be rewarded with better. Better taste, better judgment, and better capabilities.

In the words of Steve Martin: "I had no talent. None."

87. Where Is Your Hour?

If you want to get in shape, it's not difficult. Spend an hour a day running or at the gym. Do that for six months or a year. Done.

That's not the difficult part.

The difficult part is becoming the kind of person who goes to the gym every day.

And so it is with finding your voice. The tactics, the writing prompts, the kind of pencil—none of them matter compared to one simple thing: trusting yourself enough to be the kind of person who engages in the process of delivering creative work.

You manage to find an hour every day to bathe, to eat, to commute, to watch Netflix, to check your email, to hang out, to swipe at your phone, to read the news, to clean the kitchen . . .

Show us your hour spent on the practice and we'll show you your creative path.

You already know what to do to be creative.

And you already know how to do it.

You've done it before, at least once.

At least once you've said or done something insightful, generous, and original. At least once you've solved a problem or given someone a hand by shining a light.

The practice simply asks you to do it more than once, to do it often enough that it becomes your practice.

88. But Not a Hack

In London, there's a borough called Hackney. Centuries ago, when the city was much less developed, Hackney was actually on the outskirts of town, a small village that specialized in raising horses.

Not racehorses or show horses. Regular horses. Cheap horses for cheap customers. Horses that were good enough to sell, but no better.

Those horses often got purchased to pull taxi carriages. And so the nickname for London cabbies was born: hacks.

Today, a hack isn't something you want to be. A hack reverse-engineers all the work, barely getting by. The hack has no point of view, no assertions to be made. It's simply "what do you need?"

hack

professional

persistently serving your audience

no artistic vision or integrity

honoring the muse with a point of view

quest for lucky break

failure

amateur

and "how little do I have to charge to get this gig?" (or "how much can I get away with?").

It's possible (and admirable, and even heroic) to be an amateur. The amateur serves only herself. If there are bystanders, that's fine, but as an amateur your work is only for you. A privilege, a chance to find joy in creation.

And you may choose to make the leap to be a professional, to have a practice. To show up when the muse isn't there, to show up if you don't feel like it. This manifesto is for you.

But please, avoid the path of becoming a hack. Sure, work can be better than no work, but the posture of giving up your standards to get that work can quickly become toxic.

Once you see that you don't need a lucky break and that the practice is available to anyone who is willing to commit, you may choose the life of a professional. Or you can embrace the path of the engaged amateur. But the choice is a fork in the road. *A professional is not simply a happy amateur who got paid.*

89. It's Not a Paradox

But it's not easy either.

Go too far to please the audience and you become a hack. Lose your point of view, lose your reason for doing the work, become a hack. Focus only on the results, become a hack.

On the other hand, if you ignore what you see and simply create for yourself, you've walked away from empathy. If there is no change, there is no art. The professional understands the fine line between showing up with a generous vision and showing up trying to control the outcome.

The best way through the paradox is by working.

Ship creative work. On a schedule. Without attachment and without reassurance.

90. Walking Away from Being a Hack

"Deliberately. . . . When she found out she was going over people's heads, she went further, deliberately, the truth is she went right over people's heads."

DAVID CROSBY ON JONI MITCHELL

And that's why we revere Joni Mitchell forty years later and barely remember what else was on the radio those days.

Artists don't simply look in the rearview mirror, nor do they only play requests. While Mitchell was recording one of her live albums, the audience started calling out requests. She wondered aloud whether people ever asked Van Gogh to paint a *Starry Night* again.

"You have two options," she told *Rolling Stone*, "You can stay the same and protect the formula that gave you your initial success. They're going to crucify you for staying the same. If you change, they're going to crucify you for changing. But staying the same is boring. And change is interesting. So of the two options," she concluded cheerfully, "I'd rather be crucified for changing."

Leaders make art and artists lead.

91. Generous Doesn't Mean Free

Too often, the market pushes creators to give away their work. And too often, we come to believe that giving it away, removing money from the interaction, is the most generous thing we can do.

But that's not the case.

Money supports our commitment to the practice. Money permits us to turn professional, to focus our energy and our time on the work, creating more impact and more connection, not less.

And more importantly, money is how our society signifies enrollment. The person who has paid for your scarce time and scarce output is more likely to value it, to share it, and to take it seriously.

Generous doesn't require us to reduce friction by making things free. It requires us to bring bravery and passion and empathy to the people we seek to serve. And that often requires tension on the part of the audience.

It's tempting to hide by creating deniability. "What did you expect, it was free . . ."

But often, the act of charging for the work creates a generous outcome, because our work is to effect change, not to make ourselves invisible and free.

92. In Search of Enrollment

In an economy based on connection instead of industry, most of what we seek isn't actually scarce. People spend more than half their waking hours online now, in search of digital connection, entertainment, and access.

So what's worth charging for? And what do people pay for?

If you're leading, you're searching for enrollment. For people who say "I see you and trust you and want to go where you are going."

This is not what happens in compulsory education. People are there because they have to be, not because they want to be. They're there for an education (and a certificate), not for learning or passion or magic.

When we are generous with our work, we have the chance to earn trust and attention, and if we're fortunate, we will find the people who are ready to go on our journey. Those people will eagerly pay, because what we offer them is scarce and precious.

93. Toward Idiosyncrasy

The word "peculiar" comes from the idea of private property. Your cattle, to be specific. No one gets to control your livestock other than you. It's private property.

No property is more private than your voice. Your dreams and fears and contributions are yours—peculiar to you, idiosyncratic.

The industrialized economy, which is now drawing to a close, was mostly about hiding your peculiarity. It was organized around cogs, replaceable parts, and the endless drive to fit in as much as possible.

If you had a voice, you were encouraged to lower it. If we wanted your opinion, we would have asked for it. If you wanted to make change, you should keep that desire to yourself.

We've just flipped this upside down.

Today, the best work and the best opportunities go to those who are hard to replace. The linchpins, the ones who are likely to be missed.

And, delightfully, at the very same time that the economy is rewarding idiosyncrasy, we're discovering that it's also the way we were meant to be.

Because being peculiar is natural. And being peculiar is beneficial.

All change comes from idiosyncratic voices. When you bring

work from outside the status quo to people who need it, you're doing something peculiar: specific, identifiable, and actionable.

94. Choose Your Clients, Choose Your Future

The masses aren't the point. They might be a welcome side effect of your work, but to please the masses, you must pander to average.

Because mass means average.

When we decide that the change we seek to make is dependent on mass popularity, when we chase a hit, we end up sacrificing our point of view.

On average, every population is dull. The slide toward average sands off all the interesting edges, destroying energy, interest, and possibility.

What's the difference between Chip Kidd, the extraordinarily successful book cover designer, and someone with the same tools and skills that Chip has?

Chip has better clients.

Better clients demand better work. Better clients want you to push the envelope, win awards, and challenge their expectations. Better clients pay on time. Better clients talk about you and your work.

But finding better clients isn't easy, partly because we don't trust ourselves enough to imagine that we deserve them.

Every gig-economy hustler who's listed on Fiverr or Upwork or 99designs is looking for easy clients. Easy in and easy out, but they're not better clients than they have now.

Years ago, I produced a record for a very skilled duo. They were incredibly hardworking and committed to their art. In order to survive, they performed three hundred days a year, and they lived in a van, driving each day to a new town, playing at a local coffeehouse, sleeping in the van, then repeating it all the next day.

In most towns, there are a few places like this—if you've issued a few CDs and are willing to work for cheap, you can get booked without too much trouble.

These cafés are not good clients. Easy in, easy out, next!

What I helped these musicians understand is that going from town to town and working with easy gigs was wasting their effort and hiding their art. What they needed to do was stay in one town, earn fans, play again, earn fans, move to a better venue, and do it again. And again.

Working their way up by claiming what they'd earned: fans.

95. Where Are the Great Architects?

There are more than one hundred thousand licensed architects in the United States. Most of them signed up for the steady work of industrialized production. They were trained to build reliable, consistent, and efficient buildings.

Some, though, chose to see a different pattern for their work. They became architects to invent, to create, and to challenge the status quo. They are committed to building structures that invoke awe or wonder. If you've been in a building created by one of these architects, you're likely to remember it.

What's missing in this gap between good and great is the simple truth that you can't be a great architect unless you have great clients.

And at the same time, great clients rarely seek out architects who desire to be only good.

When the client wants a cheap, easy building, the architect's desire to do great work is rarely achieved. And when the client wants something important, she knows that hiring a merely good architect is a mistake.

It's tempting to blame the clients. But the commitment to be a great architect also requires the professionalism to do the hard work of getting better clients.

96. The Magic of Better Clients

Better clients are demanding. They demand more rigorous deadlines, but they also pay more. They demand extraordinary work, but they're more respectful. And they demand work they can proudly share with others. Better clients also have good taste.

You know that better clients exist; you've seen them out in the world.

The trick is earning them.

You don't do that by doing better work for lousy clients. That's because lousy clients don't want you to do better work. They are lousy clients for a reason. They don't want better work. They want a cheap commodity, or something popular. They want to cut corners, or ignore deadlines, or avoid the risk of doing something new.

You earn better clients by becoming the sort of professional that better clients want. It's lonely and difficult work. It's juggling—throw and throw, and one day, the catching will take care of itself.

Intent

97. Our Intent Matters

What change do you seek to make? Why bother to speak up or take an action if you're not seeking to change someone or something?

It makes some people deeply uncomfortable to imagine that their work will change someone else. What right, we wonder, do we have to take that on? What authority do we have to show up with any intent at all?

If there's no intent, it's likely that there's no change either. If there's no intent, it's unlikely that things will get better.

The practice becomes ever clearer: if you care enough to make change, it helps to be clear about the change you seek to make. Signing your work and owning its impact are part of the generous act of being creative.

98. Intentional Action Is Design with Purpose

Who are you trying to change?

What change are you trying to make?

How will you know if it worked?

Three simple questions, all easily avoided.

We avoid them because purpose has a flip side, and the flip side is failure.

Painting your house has a purpose. If you finish the job and your house looks terrible, then you've done a poor job. We're okay with this risk, though, because almost all house painting interventions pay off. Painting a house usually works. We don't mind establishing the purpose of painting the house early on, because it's rare we'd simply do it for fun.

If it's worth doing, it's worth establishing why we're doing it.

And once we establish why we're doing it, we're on the hook to keep our commitment.

99. Intentional Action Is Also Design with Empathy

We're not simply doing this work for ourselves. We're doing it to help someone else, to make a change happen.

That's why the "who" is so important.

Because someone who lives five thousand miles away has no stake in how we paint our house. They'll never see it or interact with it. It's not for them.

If your spouse wants the house to be painted pink and your neighbor hates pink, there's a choice to be made.

Who's the work for?

It might be possible to please everyone, but courageous art rarely tries.

Richard Serra doesn't make sculptures for people who don't like conceptual and contemporary art.

Tiffany's doesn't make rings for people who think expensive jewelry is a rip-off.

We seek to create a change for the people we serve. The most effective way to do that is to do it on purpose.

100. How Deep Does Your Empathy Run?

Some intuitive artists simply work for themselves. They bet that if the work moves them, it will move someone like them. They don't have to extend themselves at all, because there's already a successful alignment between their taste and needs and those they seek to change.

If that's already working for you, congratulations. You're one of the few. Professionals don't usually have this luxury.

It's worth noting that this isn't a moral choice, it's simply a practical one. If you're committing to the process, you'll need to choose. Choose who it's for and what it's for. And the more different the person you serve is from you, the more empathy you'll need to create the change you seek to make.

101. Who's It for?

I'll spot you this: your wishes are pure, the change is important, and it's going to make things better.

And you probably believe that things would be better if everyone got on board.

But everyone won't.

Everyone won't hear you. They won't understand you. And most of all, they won't act.

Eventually, they might come around. Some of everyone, anyway.

Sooner or later, the culture changes.

But not because you brought everyone an idea. Because their

friends and family and colleagues did. That's how widespread change always happens.

First from the source, but mostly from the sides.

102. Who Can You Reach?

How is it possible for three cowboys to herd a thousand cattle?

Easy. They don't.

They herd ten cattle, and those cattle influence fifty cattle and those cattle influence the rest.

That's the way every single widespread movement/product/ service has changed the world.

And so we ignore all the others. We ignore the masses and the selfish critics and those in love with the status quo.

First, find ten. Ten people who care enough about your work to enroll in the journey and then to bring others along.

103. You Can't Reach Everyone

But you can choose who you'll reach. If you change those people in a remarkable way, they'll tell the others.

And so begins "who's it for?"

Once you choose which subgroup to tell your story to, which subgroup needs to change, this group becomes your focus.

What do they believe?

What do they want?

Who do they trust?

What's their narrative?

What will they tell their friends?

The more concise and focused you are at this stage, the more likely it is that you're actually ready to make change happen.

Empathy again. The practical empathy of creating work that resonates with the people you seek to serve.

104. More and More Specific, Please

And so the trap. The trap is in the generic. In the cloudy persona, the undetermined person, the vague generality.

Your change is too important to be wasted on *most people*.

Which people?

Precisely which people?

What do they believe? Who has hurt them, double-crossed them, disappointed them? Who inspires them, makes them jealous? Who do they love, and why?

"Voters" is not specific. "The Lane family in rural West Virginia" is specific.

(An aside: If this is so obvious, if it's been stated for decades, if our media culture is based on it, why is it so hard for the individual creator to embrace? Because it puts us on the hook. If the

Lane family is who we made it for and the Lane family rejects it, well, that's pretty devastating. Easier, it seems, to be more generic. Easier, but less effective.)

People who like things like this will love what I'm doing.

105. Who's It for?

Who is David Byrne's next album for? Is it for the person who listened to "Burning Down the House" on the radio in 1983, or is it for the diehard fan who bought his last three albums?

Who is Fashion Week for? Is it for the working woman who is looking for something sharp to wear next week, or is it designed to attract the attention of a hundred journalists and trendsetters?

Who is this PowerPoint for? Is it supposed to change the minds of everyone in the meeting? Is it to create a paper trail so that six months from now, the boss will be able to tell everyone that they had been warned? Or is it to engage the pedants while they spend time having an emotion-based argument with the CEO?

Who is the Hermès Birkin bag for? What about Fox News? Who is donating to the United Way? Room to Read?

It's not for everyone.

Okay, that's obvious.

What about your project, your gig, your organization? Who's it for?

Once we know who it's for, it's easier to accept that we have the ability and responsibility to bring positive change to that person. Not to all people, not to create something that is beyond criticism, but for this person, this set of beliefs, this tribe.

Once you can put yourself on the hook to commit to who you are serving, you can find the empathy to make something for them.

106. Serving the Work

The process of intentional action requires us to set aside what we need so that we can focus on what the work needs. The work itself is our client and we owe it something.

This commitment can get out of hand. If we find ourselves out of balance, unable to sustain the effort, the work will suffer.

But too often we find ourselves at the other extreme, seeking confidence or personal gratification and forgetting why we created the work in the first place.

The work is your client. It's hired you to help you make a change happen. Getting paid for our work can confuse us, because it might seem that all we need to do is serve the person with a checkbook. But that's the strategy of a hack—and it rarely leads to the contributions we set out to make in the first place.

There's a tension, the gap between what the work wants and what the person paying for it wants. Dancing in that gap is the work of creating our art.

On one hand, the self, your *self*, has a vision for a possible future. On the other, the person you're seeking to serve and lead brings a set of expectations and desires to your work. The two will never be perfectly aligned, and this friction is the place where your work can thrive.

When someone needs a drill bit, we can hand them a drill bit. But if someone wants to explore a new frontier, they're going to need our help finding a creative way forward. And that's where your point of view and your contribution live.

We push on behalf of the work, and when we do, we may find that the next customer is even more eager to enroll in the journey we seek to lead.

107. Someone, Not Everyone

If you're building a bass guitar or growing an orchid or selling an electric SUV, why are you concerned with what *everyone* thinks about it?

It seems to me that you should only care about the opinions of those who are actually open to engaging with one.

Someone, not everyone.

And now that you have a circle of believers, how can you bring the best version of the work to them? Instead of compromising your way to a set of mediocre elements, how can you use this smaller group to challenge you to go in the other direction instead? Toward better instead of more?

It turns out that the believers are tired of being ignored and they're eager to cheer you on.

But first, you have to walk away from the others.

108. Crossing Economic Boundaries

Imagine how difficult it is to do college fundraising. You're getting paid just over minimum wage and you're busy trying to get two-million-dollar donations from billionaires.

As you're describing the building you'd like them to name after themselves, you're probably thinking, "This is nuts. If I had two million dollars, there's no way in the world I'd spend it to name a building after myself."

This is selfish thinking, thinking that comes from a lack of empathy and an understandable lack of experience in walking in the shoes of a billionaire.

A more generous approach would be: "This person is a billionaire. He has every toy, every house, every plane he could ever hope for. What he might be missing is status and legacy. What might mean more to him than anything he could get right now is the knowledge that for the next hundred years, generations of smart, up-and-coming young people will be saying his name. For him, two million dollars is a bargain."

Seen that way, our hesitation is hiding. We're hiding because we're afraid, because we don't see the world the way the person we're working with does.

At the other end of the spectrum, consider the social entrepreneur who is bringing solar lanterns or clean water to a rural village that's off the grid. In the mind of the entrepreneur, this is an irresistible product to offer. For less than a dollar a day, a family can have clean water, avoid getting sick, and save the hours they currently spend fetching the water they live on. Or, just as compelling, for a fee equal to what they spend on a month's worth of kerosene, that same family can have a solar lantern that lasts for two years, is brighter, cleaner, and also charges their cell phone.

And yet.

And yet few people buy either one. Because in her excitement, the entrepreneur has failed to see the world the way the prospect does.

Maybe the fear of a new technology is sufficient for someone to hesitate and wait until the neighbors go first.

Maybe respect for parents and elders means that the villager doesn't want to abandon tradition so quickly.

Maybe the status that comes with going first makes the villager uncomfortable. Or maybe it's not seen as status at all, but an apparent foolhardy recklessness that lowers status.

The process of shipping creative work demands that we truly hear and see the dreams and desires of those we seek to serve.

After understanding what our people want, we have a choice. We can build with empathy and work with their dreams, or we can choose to move on, to determine the vision is not for them, and to make something else for someone else.

To cause change to happen, we have to stop making things for ourselves and trust the process that enables us to make things for other people. We need the practical empathy of realizing that others don't see what we see and don't always want what we want.

109. What's It for? The Second Question . . .

Once we've established the change, made assertions and figured out the who, our work begins with another simple question, repeated recursively, until we figure out the next step.

What is this element of our project for?

This is intentional action.

Every element has a purpose. If you don't even know what it is, how will you do the work to achieve it?

Again, it's easy to decide to avoid being clear about the "what's it for." If you announce what something is supposed to do, it's difficult to avoid a feeling of failure when it doesn't do what you said it was going to do.

At one extreme, engineering school is filled with talented

builders who will proudly inform you that this bridge will definitely not fall down. It's math.

While at the same time, a writer's colony often has too many nascent novelists unsure whether or not their book is going to work. That's because there's no math involved. And in the absence of math, it's easy to weasel our way around the purpose of what we set out to do.

But just because we can't be sure doesn't mean we shouldn't try.

110. What Engineers Know

Everything has a function. Every element of the bridge or the spaceship is there for a reason, even if the reason is decorative.

When NASA engineers put together the payload for an Apollo rocket, they had total clarity about tradeoffs.

Everything weighs something, everything takes up space. Nothing goes on a lunar module unless there's a really good reason.

Intentional action demands a really good reason. Find a who, make an assertion, and execute your work to deliver on that promise.

You can't find a good reason until you know what you're trying to accomplish.

111. Simple Example: The Receptionist

Every day, hundreds of thousands of people go to work as receptionists.

They sit behind a desk, greet visitors, and do what receptionists have always done.

But what's it for?

After all, with electronic buzzers, cell phones, and PBXs, there's really no requirement that a human sit at the front desk all day. Plenty of companies no longer have a receptionist.

Being a pretty good receptionist is easy. You're basically a low-tech security guard in nice clothes. Sit at the desk and make sure that visitors don't steal the furniture or go behind the magic door unescorted.

But what if you wanted to be a great receptionist?

If we define the contribution of the receptionist in terms of the "what's it for," then becoming a great contributor is straightforward.

I'd start with understanding that in addition to keeping unescorted guests away from the magic door, a receptionist can have a huge impact on the marketing of an organization. If someone is visiting your office, they've come for a reason—to sell something, to buy something, to interview, or be interviewed. No matter what, there's some sort of negotiation involved. If the receptionist can influence the mindset of the guest, good things happen (or, if it goes poorly, bad things).

Think the job acceptance rate goes up if the first impression is a memorable one? Think the tax auditor might be a little more friendly if the receptionist's greeting is cheerful?

So, a great receptionist starts by acting like Vice President, Reception. They could request a small budget for bowls of M&Ms or the occasional Heath bar for a grumpy visitor. Or, to be really amazing, how about baking a batch of cookies every few days? I'd ask the entire organization for updates on who is coming in each day. "Welcome, Mr. Mitchell. How was your flight in from Tucson?"

Is there a TV in reception? Why not stream some old *Three Stooges* or *Prisoner* episodes?

Why do I need to ask where to find the men's room? Perhaps you could have a little sign.

And in the downtime between visitors, what a great chance to surf the web for recent positive news about your company. You can collate it in a little binder that I can read while I'm waiting. Or create a collage of local organizations your fellow employees have helped with their volunteer work.

One amazing receptionist I met specialized in giving sotto voce commentary on the person you were going to meet. She'd tell you inside dope that would make you feel prepared before you even walked in. "Did you know that Don had a new grandchild enter the family last week? She's adorable. Her name is Betty."

Now that it's clear what the reception job is for, it's significantly easier to do it well.

Because like just about everything we do, it's not merely a job. *It's for something.*

Of course, the objections are obvious. Most of them come down to trust. Either the boss doesn't trust the receptionist to be better than average, or more likely, the receptionist doesn't trust himself or herself enough to claim this spot.

112. Welcome to the Green Mill

If you close your eyes and visualize the perfect Chicago dive bar, you might be imagining the Green Mill. Every square inch is exactly what you would expect. It even has patina on its patina.

On Monday nights, though, the bar is transformed. At 9:00 p.m., the manager steps onto the little stage and shushes the crowd. Most of the people there already know what's going on—some of them came from as far away as Mumbai to hear Patricia Barber and her trio play jazz tonight.

For the newcomers, the rules are clear: Monday is Patricia's night, and if you're not here to listen to the music, this is a really good time to leave. Because for the next five hours, a small group of people will commune with possibility. They'll watch a jazz group at the very top of its game taking huge leaps and risks, in real time.

A legendary jazz musician like Patricia can sell out the Jazz Standard in New York. What's she doing in this tiny bar in Chicago? Perhaps a hundred people can cram in to hear her, and they do, almost every Monday year-round.

Patricia explains that this is her living room. Her people are here. Not tourists or celebrity-hunters, but jazz insiders. People who are on the journey that Patricia wants to lead.

Patricia doesn't have to worry about making a mistake in her work at the Green Mill. It's not going to show up on social media. And she doesn't have to keep her songs short, or upbeat, or in a major key either.

Patricia is here for the music, and so is the audience.

The alignment of the who and the what are the first step. The enrollment of the people in the room permits her to get right to work. And so the music is possible because Patricia has created the conditions where it can thrive.

113. Six Simple Examples of the Question

On this expensive bicycle, what's the carbon-fiber wheel for?

What's the headline for in this magazine ad?

What's the save button for on this word processor?

What's the airport announcement about security alerts for?

What is the "letters to the editor" section of the newspaper for?

What is a large front lawn on a suburban McMansion for?

If you think hard about these questions, you might discover that a lot of what we build or encounter isn't about what we think it is.

In fact, the front wheel of the expensive bicycle exists to remind the purchaser that his money was well spent. This might mean it's loud or exotic-looking or fragile. Being dramatically faster and sturdier is possible, but not required.

The headline in the magazine ad exists to get the right person to keep reading (and to have the wrong person turn the page). Beyond that, the headline is designed to put the reader into the right state of mind so the next paragraph has a chance of getting under the reader's skin.

The airport announcements are for familiarity, not attention. They exist to create a sonic background that makes the airport feel like an airport. Or perhaps they exist to give the bureaucrats deniability or the feeling of taking action.

The "letters to the editor" section of the paper is designed to

create the illusion that the editors care about what readers think. Particularly the readers who like to write letters to the editor.

And the front lawn of a typical suburban house exists as a show of willful waste. The nonproductive (and expensive) nature of the lawn itself is the point.

114. Should a Word Processor Have a Save Button?

If the software's design exists to make the new user feel comfortable, then it ought to work exactly like the software he's used to. The purpose of the save button is to reassure the new user that it's going to be okay around here.

But if the design exists to solve the word-processing problems of a committed user, then there shouldn't even be a save button. That's because the purpose of a word processor is to enable people to write, and saving that work is a key element of that task. The software is smart enough to save it all by itself. And hard disk space is cheap enough that we can save hundreds of versions, meaning that remembering to save the document is no longer part of what the user has to do.

Going one step further, it's entirely plausible that the "what's-it-for" of the software design is so generous and thoughtful that users can't help but tell their peers about the software—the design of the software is the marketing of the software. In that case, in

every interaction the software has with the user, the "what's-it-for" is to be breathtakingly smart and remarkably powerful.

Not only that, but it needs to create a sharing dynamic, one that sucks other users in and makes the software work better precisely because it's being shared.

Software like this, then, either exists to be the usual kind and mostly invisible, or it exists to spread the word through delight and connection.

Two different paths, each of which requires the architect of the project to be clear to the team, up front, about what's supposed to happen here.

115. But Wait, What about the Dance Recital?

It's one thing for a software engineer to engage in the iterative process of who and what and why, but what about those sensitive folks who have chosen to work in the arts?

A hundred years ago, Sonia Delaunay established her reputation as a contemporary artist. The pioneer of the Orphism school of painting, she changed the way people saw color and geometry in modern art. She walked away from the standards of naturalism and a traditional approach in her art, then leapt into expanding the way cubism and color could come together to make change happen.

"About 1911 I had the idea of making for my son, who had just been born, a blanket composed of bits of fabric like those I had seen in the houses of Ukrainian peasants. When it was finished, the arrangement of the pieces of material seemed to me to evoke cubist conceptions and [I] then tried to apply the same process to other objects and paintings."

Unstated was her commitment to create change with her work. Instead of seeking to fit in, she made the choice to stand out. Instead of making paintings to please the skeptics, she made art for people who were enrolled in the path toward the new. She understood the genre in which she worked, the people who were interested in it, and the venues where it could be seen and appreciated.

Delaunay was as intentional as any engineer, architect, or software designer.

116. Seeking Unlimited Emotional Authority

Totie Fields was angry. And she was focusing all of her anger on me and my mom.

It's not easy to be a stand-up comic, harder still if you're a woman and it's 1973.

In 1973, Totie was one of the most famous female comedians in the United States, appearing on Carol Burnett and the late-night talk shows. That got her a gig at a big venue in Buffalo, where I grew up. My mom, certainly unaware of what was to come, brought me along.

Her act wasn't anything like what she did on TV. She worked blue. By today's standards, I'm sure it was pretty tame, but my mom was sort of aghast. Twenty minutes into the show, seeing other parents shepherding their kids out of the theater, we got up to leave.

As we neared the exit, Fields stopped her act and shouted, "Turn up the house lights."

Like the convicts caught in the spotlight in every prison-escape movie ever made, the two of us froze.

Totie spent the next few minutes (though to us, it felt like an hour) laying into us about our failure to understand her act, how hard she was working, and how rude we were to not stay for the whole show.

Totie Fields wanted every single person in the room to feel what she wanted us to feel.

That's a mistake, of course: you can't command people to feel what you want them to feel.

All we can do is choose the right people, bring them the right work in the right way with the right intent, and then leave it to them to shift their emotional states.

We have to trust ourselves and then we have to trust the people we serve.

The trust will be repaid many times over.

117. Fear and the Muse and Your Work and Your Service

It's so tempting to avoid the *what*.

In fact, the most honest justification for not answering "what's it for?" is "I'm afraid."

And that's the best reason to ask the question. To discover that while we believe we're working toward a goal, the goal of whatever the work is ostensibly for, what we're actually doing is hiding.

Hiding takes many forms, because the source of our creativity sometimes feels as though it might flicker out if we look at it too closely. So it bobs and weaves and conceals itself whenever it can.

There's nothing wrong with choosing to go to a conference to have fun, or to hide out from work. But if the "what's-it-for" is to advance your connections and trust within the industry, sitting in the back row and offering no connection to anyone can only be described as a failure.

The "what's-it-for" recursion lets you choose to go to work, efficiently working toward a goal, whenever you decide it's important enough to ask the question.

And it permits us to be open to useful feedback.

If you're going to Huntsville, it's okay to ask for directions. You're not offended if someone tells you that you've taken a wrong turn. It's not personal and it's not devastating. It's simply helpful advice on how to get where you're going.

That's not going to happen if you're unwilling to tell us where you're hoping to go.

118. You Can See the Paradox

On one hand, we have to ignore the outcome, the box office numbers, and the famous critics, because if we obsess about them, we will break our process, lose our momentum and eventually be sapped of our will to be creative.

On the other hand, there actually is a difference between good work and not-good work. There's a point to our effort, and the change we seek to make involves empathy for others, not just the solipsism of doing whatever we feel like.

That paradox is at the heart of our practice: we must dance with it, not pretend it doesn't exist.

119. Subconscious Pre-Filtering

It's entirely possible to believe that your ideas come from the muse and your job is simply to amplify them. And that successful people are lucky because the muse keeps giving them useful and powerful ideas.

I'm not sure that's what successful people do. All of us get an endless supply of ideas, notions, and inklings. Successful people, often without realizing it, ignore the ones that are less likely to "work," and instead focus on the projects that are more likely to advance the mission.

Sometimes we call this good taste.

It's possible to get better at this pre-filtering. By doing it out loud. By writing out the factors that you're seeking, or even by explaining to someone else how your part of the world works.

Instinct is great. It's even better when you work on it.

120. What's It for?

We have a meeting at 4:00 p.m.

Okay, what's it for?

Well, we always have this meeting . . .

So, the "what's-it-for" is: It's easier to maintain the status quo than to risk not having the meeting. What the meeting is for is making sure that the people who like having the meeting aren't upset.

121. Adopting the Design-First Mindset of Intention

Mindfulness is healthy, it's professional, and it allows us to be our best self.

It is also maddeningly difficult, particularly in a culture that prizes busyness over just about everything else.

But mindful isn't the opposite of busy.

Mindfulness demands intention. Mindfulness is the practice of simply doing the work. Without commentary, without chatter, without fear.

To simply do our work.

The easiest way to achieve this is to be clear about the purpose of the work. Because if the purpose is to follow a process (something that is under our control), we can focus on the process, not on the uncertainty that distracts us.

I got a note from a reader, Gina, a little while ago. She wrote, "On a personal note—In 2016, your book *The Dip* helped me realize I was only trying to create a business so I could have the time to be a writer. I cut out the middleman and went all in on writing. Within two years I was able to become a freelance writer and researcher/fact-checker for kids and adults, full-time."

The lesson here is simple: By bringing her focus back to the purpose of the work, Gina was able to get back to work. To the work she wanted to do all along.

We do our best work with intention.

122. What's It for?

We have a new ad campaign.

Fabulous, what's it for?

Well, we have great actors, and a new logo, and wait until you hear the soundtrack.

Sure, that's fun and it looks like a lot of effort went into it, but what's it for?

Our goal is to get more shoppers into stores.

Got it. How does this ad do that?

123. Toddlers Don't Get It

Hey, little kid, why are you crying? What's the tantrum for?

He has no idea. He's a toddler. The toddler is authentic.

The hallmark of the unmindful is to react, to lash out, to spend time with no purpose or measure.

Each of us has worked with intention at least a little. The opportunity is to turn it from an occasional accident into a regular practice.

We can return again and again to this simple narrative:

1. This is a practice.

2. It has a purpose.

3. I desire to create change.

4. The change is for someone specific.

5. How can I do it better?

6. Can I persist long enough to do it again?

7. Repeat.

124. What's It for?

The TSA rule is really clear: you can't put your belt in the same bin as your laptop.

Sure, but what's it for?

It's to make flying safer.

Really? How does keeping my belt out of the bin make flying safer?

Well, it's actually to create a regime of obedience and random anxiety, which makes some people feel safer when they fly.

Oh, got it. In that case, carry on.

125. Authenticity Is a Trap

Some seek to find a posture of trust by using a simple approach: say what feels real to you. Share your innermost feelings, be yourself, and most of all be authentic.

Not only will this lead to heartbreak, it's also impossible.

There is nothing authentic about the next thing you're going to say or do or write. It's simply a calculated effort to engage with someone else, to contribute, or to cause a result.

The politician who offends everyone in the room and blows up his career may claim he was being authentic, but the choices that led to that moment were all intentional acts. This time, the actions didn't lead to the outcome he was hoping for (or perhaps they did).

The stand-up comic isn't being authentic. It's not a natural act to stand on stage with a microphone. And the chef who cooks one cuisine or another might be having fun, but it's not more authentic for him to cook eggs than it is to cook chicken (but of course, you need to cook eggs first).

If you're using any sort of self-control (there's that "self" word again), then you're not being authentic. Only a tantrum is authentic. Everything else we do with intention.

If we're going to act with intention and empathy, our path is clear. The work is to make change happen. If we don't ship the work, no change will happen. If we ship the wrong work to the wrong people, no change will happen.

Your audience doesn't want your authentic voice. *They want your consistent voice.*

126. Consistency Is the Way Forward

Not sameness. Not repetition. Simply work that rhymes. That sounds like you. We make a promise and we keep it.

No one knows exactly what movie Greta Gerwig will make next. But her fans will go see her next movie, because she directed it. She earned those fans by seeing them, understanding them, and helping them change. The promise is a significant one, and it leads to a connection between the artist and those who are served by the art.

I'm guessing that Greta Gerwig didn't make *Little Women* because she wanted to watch that movie alone in a room; she made it because she thought others would want to watch it. And by making it, she earned the right to put her name on it.

You don't want an authentic heart surgeon ("I don't care if you're having a fight with your landlord—do the surgery as if today's your very best day") or even an authentic chef ("I don't care that you don't feel like cooking Mexican tonight. It's on the menu and that's what I ordered").

What we seek out is someone who sees us and consistently keeps their promises to bring us the magic we were hoping for. Someone who has committed to rhyming with what they did yesterday.

When you trust yourself enough to turn pro, you're entering into a covenant with those you seek to serve. You promise to design with intention, and they agree to engage with the work you promised to bring them.

127. Realer Than Real

Steven Pressfield wrote, "What have you and I been put on this Earth to do? Is it not the creation of the 'inauthentic,' that is the purposefully crafted, in order to deliver to others the gift and simulacrum of authenticity? That's why they call it Art, and why, in some crazy way, it's realer than real and truer than true."

Realer than real and truer than true.

That's the authentic we seek.

That's the work of creation. To invent something, not to discover it.

Steven and I couldn't agree more about authenticity. But it's still a powerful place to hide.

We can only deliver what our audience needs by being consistent, by creating our inauthentic, intentional, crafted art in a way that delivers an authentic experience to our audiences as they consume it.

Did the word "inauthentic" make you bristle? That's how good a job the creators of the mythology of creativity have done in brainwashing us. We have lots of words for people who are proudly inauthentic. We call them professionals, champions, leaders, and heroes. It's hard to authentically show up day after day, working hour after hour, when there's probably something else you'd rather be doing. It's difficult to encounter a dangerous situation without blinking, to patiently persist in the face of criticism, or even to merely show up on a regular basis. But that difficult work is *all* inauthentic. It's work we do precisely because we don't feel like it in the short run. It's the choice to do something for long-term reasons, not because we're having a tantrum.

Inauthentic means effective, reasoned, intentional. It means it's not personal, it's generous.

The hack can't do this. The professional can choose to.

128. Intentional Action Has a Few Simple Elements

1. Determine who it's for. Learn what they believe, what they fear, and what they want.

2. Be prepared to describe the change you seek to make. At least to yourself.

3. Care enough to commit to making that change.

4. Ship work that resonates with the people it's for.

5. Once you know whom it's for and what it's for, watch and learn to determine whether your intervention succeeded.

6. Repeat.

No Such
Thing As
Writer's
Block

129. Credentialing Is a Roadblock

The education-industrial complex has grown up around the idea that no one has the ability to create useful work without a certificate.

And there are certainly many places where a credential is essential. I don't want a knee surgeon who learned the craft by watching YouTube videos.

On the other hand, you don't need a permit to speak up, to solve an interesting problem, or to lead. You don't need a degree to write a lyric, lead a cohort, or take responsibility either.

The system established credentials to maintain the consistency of our industrial output, but over time, they've been expanded to create a roadblock, a way to slow down those who would seek to make change happen.

Credentialing is a form of signaling, a stalling device, and also a way to keep diversity down.

Acting "as if" is difficult for many people, particularly because the powers that be often try to exclude noncredentialed people from the work. But again and again, they're failing.

Take a look at the leaders you respect, in any field. And then consider the credential that got them there.

If you're headed to graduate school to get a master's, you might be better off spending those two years actually doing the work instead.

130. The Curse of the Famous College

It begins with the myth that a famous college is the same thing as a good college, even though there's no evidence at all that they're related.

Famous colleges need to enforce the regime of compliance and scarcity, so they seek our cooperation and belief to build their reputation. They're only famous because we want them to be famous.

That desire is about credentialing. The magic power a famous institution has to bless us with status and authority.

You can't start a varsity football team on your own, but what about an improv troupe? A friend went to an Ivy League college, applied for the improv squad, and didn't make the cut. And so he gave up.

If we've been seduced into needing a credential to do the least credentialed art—improv—it's fair to imagine that it's endemic to our narrative.

From an early age, high achievers are taught to sacrifice independent thought for a good grade. We're taught that compliance will be rewarded by being picked. And the biggest pick for many kids is the approval that comes from a famous college (or the improv group that's running auditions at said famous college).

This desire for external approval and authority directly undermines your ability to trust yourself, because you've handed this trust over to an institution instead.

Now, more and more of us are seeing that it's a fraud. The institutions have no magical powers, as they're regularly proved wrong in their ability to select, to mold, and to amplify human beings who care enough to make change happen.

131. But What a Great Excuse

Credentialing wouldn't have the power it does if we didn't eagerly embrace our lack of a credential as the perfect place to hide.

After all, if you haven't been picked, you're off the hook.

And if you don't have the means to apply or pay for the credential, you don't even have to bother getting rejected, because you've already rejected yourself.

When the Wizard gave the Scarecrow his diploma, he didn't give him anything that he didn't already have. The paper was unnecessary external validation that helped the Scarecrow find the trust he probably could have captured on his own.

132. Any Excuse Will Do

If it works on you, if it gives you a way to stall, to interrupt your practice and to avoid the truth of your work, then it's now a good excuse. Or at least an effective one. The truth of the excuse doesn't matter . . . it worked.

To find the people who don't have a good excuse, simply look for those who have managed to make a difference. They didn't get caught by a well-engineered narrative of distraction or dismay.

By ignoring excuses, regardless of how valid they are, they've managed to get back on track and do their work.

The truth: if a reason doesn't stop everyone, it's an excuse, not an actual roadblock.

133. Fake Experts

Rejecting the trap of credentialing opens the door to fake experts. If no credential is needed, if everyone is qualified, leveraged, and able to do this job, aren't we inviting hacks and charlatans in to do important work?

I think the opposite is true. Credentialing lulls us into false confidence about who is actually an expert. The fact that you have a degree doesn't mean you have insight, experience, or concern. You've acquired a piece of paper, but that doesn't mean you care.

Actions matter more today than ever before. We can see your work, hear your words, and understand your intent.

Today, we can go beyond the credential and actually see your impact. We can create a body of work and a community that understands the impact we're capable of.

I'm not provoking you to become a charlatan (or to follow one). Simply to take the opportunity that's available to engage in the long process of earning genuine expertise, in service of making a change.

134. Steve Ballmer Cared Too Much about Being Right

Steve Blank points out that when Microsoft CEO Steve Ballmer took over from Bill Gates, he promptly began a multiyear cycle to destroy the company:

Despite Microsoft's remarkable financial performance, Ballmer failed to understand and execute on the five most important technology trends of the twenty-first century: in search—losing to Google; in smartphones—losing to Apple; in mobile operating systems—losing to Google/Apple; in media—losing to Apple/Netflix; and in the cloud—losing to Amazon.

How did he miss so consistently?

Simple: He only focused the company on what he thought Microsoft was good at. He structured the company to defend their core competencies, creating an organization that was merely competent. They optimized for the twentieth century and gave away the twenty-first century to people who were willing to fail.

Even leaders at companies can choose to believe that they are blocked.

But of course, there's no such thing as being blocked. Because being creative is a choice.

By focusing on the avoidance of error and working too hard on controlling the outcome, Ballmer walked away from the process. And so he chose to block an entire company.

135. It's Okay to Maintain the Status Quo

Many things we do are designed to make those around us feel safe, to help them trust us, or to create a foundation for other work.

The answer to the "what's-it-for" question might be "because we've always done it this way."

And as long as you're pleased with the change you've been getting, doing the same thing to get it again might be precisely the right plan.

A chef is more likely to create a remarkable meal if she maintains most of the tropes of what it means to go out for dinner.

Chicago chef Iliana Regan has won a Michelin star six years in a row. When she and her wife, Anna Hamlin, decided to move to rural Michigan to create a new sort of restaurant, they realized that the easiest way to do this was to continue calling it a restaurant, to build a traditional inn, and to bring their work to the sort of people who are used to spending money in Michelin-starred restaurants.

And precisely because the restaurant fits into an expected slot, they can challenge convention in other ways—their pricing, location, and menu are more in line with René Redzepi than with a diner down the street.

You don't have to change everything. In fact, it's likely that you can't.

136. Writer's Block

Writer's block is a myth.

Writer's block is a choice.

Writer's block is real.

And yet it's all invented.

But that doesn't mean it isn't real.

Gravity isn't invented. Everyone experiences it the same way. Chocolate isn't invented. That's either a chocolate bar or it isn't.

But writer's block is invented. So is a fear of spiders, a belief in astrology, or the confidence we feel before giving a speech.

We know this because it changes. It changes from person to person and from day to day. It's a story.

Stories are real.

And stories can change.

If your story isn't working for you, you can find a better one to take its place.

137. The Search for Certainty Is at the Heart of Our Block

In an industrial world, the high-stakes marketplace requires us to be right. Every time.

Make a mistake on the assembly line and you lose your job.

Make an error at the bank and you're out.

Say the wrong words in a meeting and get fired.

But the world we seek to create doesn't exist yet, and it has no right answers. If we knew how to do this work, we would have done it already.

To be creative is to work on the frontier, to invent the next thing, the thing for which there isn't a playbook or a manual.

Certainty, then, must be elusive, because we can't know for sure. The elusiveness isn't a problem, it's not a bug, it's not something to be eliminated.

The uncertainty is the point.

138. Polish Is Overrated

Steely Dan continues to sell records and stream near the top of their niche. A band that did their best work more than forty years ago is now a classic.

The duo behind the group, Becker and Fagan, are known for refusing to tour for years. Instead, they created and performed their work in a studio, using studio musicians, and then spent months or years polishing the recordings to a bright sheen, establishing a standard for a sort of perfection.

It's easy to think that this sort of perfectionism is the only path you should take in order to create great work. But do you know who else is still on the charts? Singers like Bruce Springsteen, Johnny Cash, and Aretha Franklin. Groups like Jefferson Airplane. Artists who never won a Grammy for polish. In fact, they were manufacturing a sort of intimate authenticity, and viewed too much shine as a defect.

The irony in Steely Dan's touring success over the last twenty years isn't lost on me. Their live shows can't possibly compare to the production values of their albums, which is the best reason to go see them.

Getting rid of your typos, your glitches, and your obvious errors is the cost of being in the game. But the last three layers of polish might be perfectionism, not service to your audience. Failure is the foundation of our work.

The process demands that we live on the frontier. That we learn new skills, explore new audiences, and find new magic for our existing audiences. As soon as we've mastered an approach or technique we begin again, in search of a new and more powerful one.

But the only way to find something new is to be prepared (or even eager) to be wrong on our way to being right.

Nintendo was a playing card company. Starbucks continues to fail at creating a viable food option in their stores. Adobe has shipped hundreds (!) of software products that failed to catch on.

The same is true for individual creators. There are entire seasons of *Seinfeld* with writing that doesn't compare to the great episodes that made it a classic. Every author you love has published at least one book you won't like very much.

The practice seeks to make change, but the process demands originality. The practice is consistent, but only in intention, not in execution.

Every creator who has engaged in the practice has a long, nearly infinite string of failures. All the ways not to start a novel, not to invent the light bulb, not to transform a relationship.

Again and again, creative leaders fail. It is the foundation of our work.

We fail and then we edit and then we do it again.

139. Aretha's Purse

At the Kennedy Center Honors in 2015, a host of all-stars joined Aretha Franklin onstage, from James Taylor to Janelle Monáe.

Also on the stage: Aretha Franklin's handbag. As the song

ended, James Taylor, wanting to be helpful, bent down to pick it up for her. Aretha practically pushed him away.

What was in the purse?

Franklin learned something about the music business the hard way: during the 1960s and 1970s, artists, particularly people of color and women, didn't always get paid for their work. "Later" meant "never."

And so she developed the habit of getting paid, in cash, before she went onstage. And of bringing the money onstage with her, in her purse.

That habit soon became a narrative.

Over the decades, her status and the industry changed, but her narrative did not. The fear of middlemen (including lawyers) probably led to her lack of a formal will, leaving a mess after she died.

All of us have a narrative—one about who to trust, or what's likely to happen next, or how to do our work.

The practice reworks our narrative into something that helps us get to where we seek to go.

140. Is the Narrative Working?

Our story is about how the world works, our role in it, and what might happen next.

It could be something as generic as "I'm a pessimist" or as specific as "No one ever chooses me because I have red hair." It's a narrative about insufficiency that leads some people to stick with a stifling job, and a narrative about appearance that leads others to needless cosmetic surgery.

Our narrative informs our choices, our commitments, and most of all, our ability to make a difference in the culture. It's the frame we use to interpret the world around us.

Two questions about your narrative:

1. Is it closely aligned to what's actually happening in the world?

If, for example, you're constantly worried about something happening, but it never does, it's probably a miscalculation on your part. If you believe your work is fabulous but no one wants to interact with it, again, you might not be telling a truthful story about the world. Here's a simple test. Ask: Do other successful people have this narrative?

2. Is it working? Is the narrative you use helping you achieve your goals? Because that's what it's for.

If it's getting in your way, then instead of trying to change the outside world to match your expectations of it, it might pay for you to change the narrative instead.

And you've already guessed: writer's block is simply a side effect of our narrative. It's not an actual physical or organic ailment, simply a story we tell ourselves, one that leads to bad work habits and persistent fear.

141. The Unblocked Architect

Mexico-based architect Alejandro de la Vega Zulueta is known for high-rise apartment buildings. To be original in architecture is an ongoing challenge because there are so many constraints and such an emphasis on utility.

In a world of sameness, he's known not just for his creativity, but also for getting it built.

To get unstuck, he starts drawing geometric shapes. And then he scans them, prints them, and turns them into three-dimensional panels. He doesn't begin with the end, he begins at the beginning. But he begins.

It's hard to get blocked when you're moving. Even if you're not moving in the direction that you had in mind that morning.

142. The Infinite Game

The infinite game is the game we play to play, not to win. James Carse coined the term, but the concept has been around since before language. Simon Sinek wrote a new classic on the topic. The infinite game is a catch in the backyard with your four-year-old son. You're not trying to win catch; you're simply playing catch.

The most important parts of our lives are games that we can't imagine winning.

The process is infinite, if we trust it to be. We don't do this work hoping that we will win and the game will be over. After Susan Kare designed the magical icons for the Mac, she didn't stop work. Instead, she designed some more—in various media, for other audiences, in other forms.

Play to keep playing.

Each step is movement on a journey that we can only hope will continue. The infinite game has no winners or losers, no time clock or scoreboard. It is simply a chance to trust ourselves enough to participate.

143. A Marathon Is an Infinite Game

Fifty-two thousand people run the New York Marathon. At least fifty-one thousand of them have no chance of winning . . . if we measure winning by the scarcity-based notion of finishing first.

The marathon we see is largely about cooperation, not direct competition. No one is elbowing anyone or sabotaging their efforts. Because the real competition is with your own potential, not with the other runners.

The marathon we don't see is the year of lonely early-morning runs, the support groups, and the persistence of effort.

That's why authors blurb one another's books. The act of creation isn't about finding scarcity that belongs to you and to no one else. The act of creation involves touching something abundant and being eager to share it with other creators.

It's hard to imagine Tim Cook blurbing a Samsung phone. That's because Apple seeks to corner the market, not to spread an idea or create a positive change. They're in the business of raising their stock price, and everything else is merely a tactic.

144. Where Do We Put the Tired?

If you run a marathon, you're going to get tired. It would make no sense to hire a coach and say, "I want you to help me train so I don't get tired when I run a marathon."

The only difference between the tens of thousands of people who finish the marathon and those that don't is that the finishers figured out where to put their tired.

And the same goes for our art.

Everyone who creates feels resistance. Everyone who is seriously engaged in the deep effort of inventing and shipping original work feels the fear.

That's not the question.

The question is: where do you put the fear?

145. The Real Lesson of Improv Begins with "Yes, and . . ."

Improv comedy done right is thrilling. It's leaping without a net, an uncalculated free-fall in which two or more people dance as the clock ticks and the fear rises. Will they connect?

The improv team (and it only works as a team, players in an infinite game) tosses the dialogue ball back and forth, raising the stakes as they weave something out of nothing.

Charna Halpern and Del Close were pioneers of modern improv. Their first rule of improv is that "no" is a buzz killer. When the energy comes to you, the answer is always "yes, and . . ."

Forward motion is the only sort of motion that we're interested in.

Take the situation you were handed, the lines that were uttered, the tension in the room, and then act as if "yes, and . . ."

Yes, this happened, AND I'm going to do something with it.

When ego shows up, when we try to control the energy instead of sharing it, we're tempted to say "no."

"No, you did it wrong."

"No" appears at the very same time that possibility fades away.

"No" is our attempt to regain control, but it means we've abandoned the process as we chase an outcome instead.

146. "Yes, and" Is Enough

The real lesson of improv is the power of uncertainty and the acknowledgment of the absurdity of writer's block. Improv keeps moving, so there's no writer's block. But there's still lousy improv, because of ego, seeking control. There is fear, putting up walls, and stopping the process. When we let the ego subside and acknowledge the fear, then we're able to say "yes, and . . ."

Here are some of the people who studied improv with Close or Halpern: Amy Poehler, Amy Sedaris, Bill Murray, Dan Aykroyd, Gilda Radner, Harold Ramis, John Belushi, John Candy, Jon Favreau, Shelley Long, Stephen Colbert, and Tina Fey.

One theory is that only very funny people made the trip to Chicago to go through the training. The other theory, the one that makes more sense to me, is that understanding the process can make you funny if you care enough.

When we stop worrying about whether we've done it perfectly, we can focus on the process instead.

Saturday Night Live doesn't go on at 11:30 p.m. because it's ready. It goes on because it's 11:30.

We don't ship because we're creative. We're creative because we ship.

Take what you get and commit to a process to make it better.

147. Anchor Up

We like to keep promises. It's hard to be a successful happy person if you don't have the habit of keeping your promises.

But some promises are more difficult to make (and keep) than others.

We hesitate to make a promise like "the show will be on at 11:30," because we're not sure we can meet the deadline *and* make it happen in a way that allows us to control the outcome.

But sometimes we make the promise anyway.

The subconscious is powerful. If it knows that we've made a promise, that the book is due, that the brainstorming session is starting, that the pitch meeting with the VC is tomorrow— our subconscious will work overtime to help us keep that promise.

Anchors can drag us down. That's their job on a boat.

But for a creative person, an anchor can also be a beacon, the thing we work toward, relentlessly.

Not because it's perfect.

But because it's 11:30.

We promised.

The process, not the outcome. That's the heart of our practice. Good process leads to good outcomes.

148. The Generous Critic

When we ship our work, the market might respond. We call market response "criticism."

It's easy to fear criticism. Because your work is personal. Because you'd like to do it some more. And mostly, because you seek to make change for those you want to serve, and criticism is a symptom that you failed.

Wouldn't it be great, we wonder, if every person loved it, unreservedly?

Worst of all, criticism reminds us of the outcomes, not the process. Criticism takes us out of our commitment to the process—this time, for some people, the work didn't work.

Most criticism shared in the internet age is useless, or worse, harmful. It's useless because it often personalizes the criticism to be about the creator, not the work. And it's useless because most critics are unskilled and ungenerous.

I stopped reading my Amazon reviews seven years ago. Partly because I have never once met an author who said, "I read all of my one-star reviews and now my work is much better."

You don't need to hear from anonymous trolls, nor do you need to worry at all about the criticism from people who don't want the sort of thing you make. All they've done is announce that they're not the ones you seek to serve.

But a generous critic? Priceless. The generous critic has taken the time to regard your work, understand your intent, and then speak up. The generous critic is ready to be enrolled in your journey, is eager to go where you'd like to take them.

That means you can learn something. And learning something is part of the process.

149. What to Say to a Generous Critic

"Thank you."

That critic just gave you a clue.

She told you what might work. Not for the market, probably, but for her and for people like her.

And if she's any good, she delivered that criticism without indicting you, without questioning your motives, your competency, or your judgment. Simply the work.

"The work didn't work. Here's what would make it work for me."

"Thank you."

150. The Non-Generous Critic

The Amazon reviews for Nell Freudenberger's book *Lost and Wanted* are inherently unhelpful. There's a two-star review that criticizes the book for having "too much science." Never mind that it's about a physicist, that it's science fiction, and that it has received raves from people who talked about how moving and intimate it was. There's another two-star review from someone who claims that he was a "physicist in academia," but that there wasn't *enough* science.

These critics have told us a lot about themselves, but nothing much about the book. They're actually helpful in one respect: they're making it really clear that this is a book for people who like books similar to this one.

And to everyone else, "It's not for you."

What we actually learn from criticism like this is whether the marketer has done a good job of finding the right audience for the work.

When you're consistent in who it's for and what it's for, you can claim the high ground and clearly say, "It's not for you."

151. Sam Raimi and the Horror of the Boos

Raimi is one of the most successful film directors of his generation (*Spiderman*, *Evil Dead*, etc.).

As a teenager and later in film school, he insisted on screening his films for a paying audience. "Fifty cents, a dollar, it didn't matter, as long as they paid *something*." He discovered early on that paying audiences cared more and demanded more.

Again and again, his work was booed and met with derision. Paying money gave you the right to boo.

So he'd go back to the editing room and edit the film. He'd make the scary parts scarier, the funny parts funnier, and then he'd do it again.

Sooner or later, Sam Raimi made movies that he was proud of.

Which was the hard part? I think it was seeking out the boos.

152. The Possibility of 1,000 True Fans

Kevin Kelly taught us about the economic power and artistic freedom of a thousand true fans. One thousand people who will drive across town for you, pay for your work in advance, or back your Patreon campaign. One thousand people who will let you sleep on their floor or pay you $200 a year for the work you do.

A solo artist can live well with a thousand true fans.

The problem is most creatives don't even have ten.

After your family and circle of friends (who have little choice in the matter), there's a wide gap before you reach the actual fans. That's because the pressure to conform and to avoid the boos pushes us away from being fan-worthy.

True fans require idiosyncrasy. True fans are looking for something peculiar, because if all they wanted was the Top 40 or the regular kind, they could find it far more easily from someone who isn't you.

153. Sunk Costs and Your Practice

Every hour you've already spent on the work is gone. Every penny you've invested is gone as well.

These are the sunk costs. The years you spent in law school. The hours you took on the first draft of the novel. The money you spent to buy this ticket or that asset.

The thing is, these are gifts. Gifts from your former self to the self of today.

Harry Harrison, creator of *Soylent Green*, spent a year of his life writing a science fiction novel about a virus that comes from outer space. A few weeks before he was going to submit it to his publisher, Michael Crichton published *The Andromeda Strain* and it became a huge hit.

Harry's book, which was fully original, was now nothing but a knockoff.

He didn't submit the book, because he didn't want the gift from his former self. Sure, he had a finished book, but the next year of his life would have been spent promoting and defending a book that wasn't going to help his readers or his career.

"No thank you."

The time and effort he had put into the book was gone. Gone if it had worked, gone if it hadn't. But now, he had new time and effort to invest. And instead of investing it in this existing project (where it would be wasted), he simply said to his former self, "that's okay, thank you, but I'm going to make something else."

If the practice you've developed isn't getting you what you are after, you can politely walk away from it. If the audience you've worked so hard to build trust with is making it clear that your vision doesn't match theirs, you can move on.

It's fine to experience regret when we abandon a sunk cost. It's a mistake to stick with one simply because we can't bear the regret.

154. Sunk Costs and Defensiveness

Shark Tank creates tension by juxtaposing entrepreneurs with a self-confident panel of judges. The entrepreneur brings an idea to the judges. The idea is real, the project is underway. It's personal, and it's urgent.

The judges, on the other hand, give off-the-cuff suggestions and seek substantial changes.

This quickly becomes a simple back and forth: "Your idea sucks" followed by, "No, it doesn't." This evolves into, "You are a bad person" followed by "No, I'm not."

It's brittle. It's brittle because the project is already underway, and even though it's a sunk cost, it's very real and it's very personal.

It's hard to be open to feedback, to be flexible, and to stay unblocked when you're busy defending the work you've already done.

The helpful critic understands this. She's more likely to say, "I love x, y, and z, and we could make the other parts even better by . . ." Because that bypasses the brittleness.

Sunk costs are real, but sunk costs must be ignored.

155. Bonus: The Forty-Five Ways

There are at least forty-five ways we sacrifice our work to our fear:

1. Stall.

2. Expand the project so it cannot move forward.

3. Shrink the project so that it doesn't matter.

4. Ship crap.

5. Don't ship work that can be improved by others.

6.   Refuse to listen to generous critics.

7.   Eagerly listen to well meaning but chickenhearted critics.

8.   Sacrifice the work for the commercial short term.

9.   Hide from deadlines.

10. Become a diva.

11. Compromise on the good parts.

12. Compromise on the hard parts.

13. Assume that inspiration lies in a bottle or a pill.

14. Don't go to work.

15. Work all the time.

16. Wait for the muse.

17. Talk about the work too early, looking for a reason to abandon it.

18. Don't talk about the work with the right people, crippling it.

19. Define the work as you and you as the work, making it all personal.

20. Work only when inspiration strikes.

21. Fall behind on domain knowledge.

22. Copy everything.

23. Copy nothing.

24. Embrace jealousy.

25. Taunt yourself.

26. Announce that the important work takes longer.

27. Expect applause.

28. Demand cash commensurate with effort or insight, and hold back until it arrives.

29. Avoid sales calls.

30. Read your reviews.

31. Memorize your reviews.

32. Respond to your reviews.

33. Catastrophize.

34. Focus on your impending or eventual death.

35. Assume immortality as a way of stalling.

36. Listen to people who are afraid.

37. Confuse perfectionism with quality.

38. Hold on tighter as the ship date approaches.

39. Let go too soon as the ship date approaches.

40. Miss ship dates on a regular basis.

41. Don't set ship dates.

42. Redefine your zone of contribution to be smaller than it needs to be, thus letting yourself off the hook.

43. Surround yourself with people who have small dreams.

44. Polish your excuses.

45. Pretend you have writer's block.

156. The Option of Vulnerability

Film icon Adam Driver said, "I don't have an instrument, I don't play the cello. It's yourself, so in a way, it's more vulnerable."

This is toxic thinking. It also belies the mindset of the professional.

Adam Driver is an *actor*. It's not "yourself," it's a role. And Jennifer Weiner is a *writer*. The words are typed, but they aren't her, they are simply her words.

Creators make stuff up.

We create.

To create art we make choices. We do it with intent, seeking to make a change for certain people. When we find that our choices didn't succeed, vulnerability with lots of personal angst is an available choice. The alternative is to learn from what didn't resonate. Was it our choices in how we did the work, or did we bring this work to the wrong audience?

You are not your work. Your work is a series of choices made with generous intent to cause something to happen.

We can always learn to make better choices.

157. Abbey Ryan, Isaac Asimov, and the Power of Typing

Abbey Ryan sits down and paints. She's produced more than a thousand paintings, a painting a day.

Isaac Asimov published more than four hundred books. How did he possibly pull that off?

Asimov woke up every morning, sat in front of his manual typewriter, and he typed.

That was his job, to type.

The stories he created, the robots and the rest, were the bonus that came along for the ride.

He typed when he wasn't inspired. The typing turned into writing and he became inspired.

We don't write because we feel like it.

We feel like it because we write.

158. Write until You're No Longer Afraid to Write

It doesn't matter whether you call yourself a "writer." It doesn't matter if you're a singer or a traffic engineer.

Write more.

Write about your audience, your craft, your challenges. Write about the trade-offs, the industry, and your genre.

Write about your dreams and your fears. Write about what's funny and what's not.

Write to clarify. Write to challenge yourself.

Write on a regular schedule.

Writing isn't the same as talking, because writing is organized and permanent. Writing puts you on the hook.

Don't you want to be on the hook?

159. Scarcity and Creativity

> *"Poetry is not like reasoning, a power to be exerted according to the determination of the will. A man cannot say, 'I will compose poetry.' The greatest poet even cannot say it."*

PERCY BYSSHE SHELLEY

This is a dangerous misconception. It lets us off the hook and creates a wall between those magically blessed to be creative and the rest of us.

What a miserly and fearful way to see the world.

The alternative is to imagine that there's an abundance of opportunity, a nearly infinite number of poems (and other acts of creative genius) that are just waiting to be contributed to the world.

If only the poet cared enough, believed enough, and tried long enough.

In fact, determination is precisely what's needed to write poetry or create art. Determination of the will opens the door for us to trust ourselves enough to actually find the words.

160. The Essential Quality of the Bogeyman

He doesn't exist.

This is what makes him the perfect creator of fear. An enemy with no defects, an affront for which there is no defense.

The bogeyman was invented hundreds of years ago. A combination of a scarecrow, a beetle, and a ghost, his job is to scare children into compliance.

Critics and skeptics can bring up the bogeyman because they know there is no acceptable response. The bogeyman of being blocked, of running dry, of having nothing to contribute. And mostly, the bogeyman of no talent.

Except for one: denying his existence.

The bogeyman doesn't exist. That's why he's such an effective example, and why you should ignore him.

Creators flee the bogeyman every day. They invent new powers for him, imagining his ability to destroy the work and derail a career. The more power you give him, the more power he has.

But only if you're afraid to look at him.

As soon as you look him in the eye, he vanishes.

161. Chop Wood and Carry Water

Layman Pang, more than a thousand years ago, wrote:

> My daily activities are not unusual,
> I'm just naturally in harmony with them.
> Grasping nothing, discarding nothing . . .
> Drawing water and chopping wood.

This is where the modern phrase "chop wood, carry water" came from. The key word, the word that's unstated, is "simply."

To do it without commentary or drama. To do it without regard for things that are out of your control. To do it without relying on the outcome being what you hoped for.

This simple Zen instruction helps us understand our work as creatives. To eliminate the externals, to dial down the drama, and to avoid special situations.

This is the practice.

Simply to chop the wood and carry the water.

Again and again.

External success only exists to fuel our ability to do the work again.

162. Mise en Place Is Its Own Reward

A skilled chef will be certain to arrange her cooking supplies before firing the stove. All the ingredients will be chopped, measured, and laid out. This prevents last-minute urgencies, but even more than that, it gives her a chance to visualize what's to come.

Seeing the tools and ingredients, ready to go, prepared with care, opens the door for intentional action.

The internet is our enemy when it comes to mise en place because we cannot see what it will bring us, unbidden, as we sit to do our work. For me, email is the trap, but it might be anything on your phone that beeps or tweets or vibrates.

The internet brings uninvited energy, positive and negative, to the work we set out to do. It opens an infinite spigot of new ideas, new tools, and new people for the project.

If you want to create your work, it might pay to turn off your wi-fi for a day. To sit with your tools and your boundaries and your process and nothing else.

There is time to engage with the world after we do our work, but right now, we fill the cup and we empty the cup. We sit and type and then we type some more.

163. But What about the Muse?

Every creative person has experienced the seduction of the muse. That golden moment when some force takes over and magic happens. It's almost as if we're not involved. Something else is controlling our voice. The muse has arrived; the gods have allowed genius to flow through us.

It's so tempting to give credit for flow to the muse. We build an altar and sacrifice whatever we need to in order to invite her back again. When the muse is missing, we feel blocked. Everything seems more difficult and the work we produce feels a bit dull.

In those moments, it's almost as if we only have two choices: follow the dull path to being a hack, or give up for the day and hope that the muse will return. Our practice is at risk, and it's tempting to simply back off.

Perhaps our altar has candles and incense. Or perhaps we drink it from a bottle. For some, the bad habits we develop in search of the muse take over our lives.

And so we avert our gaze. We tremble in her presence. We worry that we're not in the right emotional moment to do our work. And mostly, we give away our agency, begging someone, anyone, to do the hard part of summoning the muse or getting us approval or a gig or support so that we can maybe, just maybe, feel the light again.

It's a trap.

Flow is the result of effort. The muse shows up when we do the work. Not the other way around.

Set up your tools, turn off the internet, and go back to work.

164. In Search of Desirable Difficulty

As we seek to level up, it's easy to be seduced into looking for flow.

Flow is the mental state we experience when it feels like everything is fitting together. Researcher Mihaly Csikszentmihalyi talks about the feeling of flow that we have when we're completely absorbed in a challenging but doable task. This is one of those moments when the muse is with us, and it feels great.

But while it may be satisfying, it probably doesn't help us move our practice forward as much as we'd like.

UCLA professor Robert Bjork has argued that desirable difficulty is actually required for us to upskill and move to another level.

Consider two kinds of batting practice. In one, the pitches are chunked into categories—twenty-five fastballs, twenty-five curve balls—in a predictable rhythm. At the end of this practice, hitters reported feeling a sense of confidence and flow.

The alternative involves mixing up the pitches randomly. Here, the batters reported frustration and less satisfaction. But teacher

Torre' Mills points out that the random method, where desirable difficulty is at work, actually improves players' skills more than the chunked approach.

Desirable difficulty is the hard work of doing hard work. Setting ourselves up for things that cause a struggle, because we know that after the struggle, we'll be at a new level.

Learning almost always involves incompetence. Shortly before we get to the next level, we realize that we're not yet at that level and we feel insufficient. The difficulty is real, and it's desirable if our goal is to move forward.

When we intentionally avoid desirable difficulty, our practice suffers, because we're only coasting.

The commitment, then, is to sign up for days, weeks, or years of serial incompetence and occasional frustration. To seek out desirable difficulty on our way to a place where our flow is actually productive in service of the change we seek to make.

165. Batting Practice

No one criticizes the home-run hitter for taking batting practice.

At the same time, no one is surprised that 70 percent of the time, they don't even reach first base.

If you need a guarantee of critical and market success every time you seek to create, you've found a great place to hide. If the need for critical and market success has trapped you into not being bold again, you've found another place to hide.

Batting practice is a practice. Writing every day is a practice. Learning to see is a practice. You're never done, and you're never sure.

We have unlimited reasons to hide our work and only one reason to share it: to be of service.

166. Nike's Slogan Error

"Just do it" is not helpful advice.

It can be read as "what the hell" or "get it over with." Just ship it, just hand it in, just do what you can get away with . . .

A useful adjustment is to remind yourself to "*merely* do it." Merely do the work without commentary or drama or anger. Focus on the change you seek to make and bring intent to the craft. Simply that. Nothing more or less.

I'll agree that it doesn't make as powerful a TV commercial, but it's significantly more useful.

We continue to focus on process, not solely on outcomes. If the process is right, the outcome will inevitably follow.

Chop wood, carry water. Anchor up. "Yes, and." Ignore the parts you can't control.

167. You Don't Need More Good Ideas, You Need More Bad Ideas

All the good ideas must be taken by now.

Back when Dr. Seuss was writing, there were only tens of thousands of books for kids. Now, there are millions to choose from. The same is true for movie script ideas, summer camp special days, niches for surgeons, original landscaping ideas . . .

It's tempting to imagine that there's no possible way to make a contribution. The muse has passed you by and there's nothing left to create.

Instead of saying, "I'm stuck, I can't come up with anything good," it's far more effective to say, "I've finished this, and now I need to make it better." Or possibly, "I finished this, and it can't be made better, but now I'm ready to do the new thing, because look at all I've learned."

This is the story of every human innovation.

This is the story of every good idea, every new project, every pop song, every novel.

There was a bad idea.

And then there was a better one.

If you want to complain that you don't have any good ideas, please show me all your bad ideas first.

Befriending your bad ideas is a useful way forward. They're not your enemy. They are essential steps on the path to better.

168. The Smallest Viable Breakthrough

Could you rewrite one paragraph of *Fahrenheit 451* and make it better than Bradbury's version?

Could you write one new page for the screenplay of *The Matrix*?

Can you play just one note on the clarinet that's worth listening to?

Instead of focusing on a masterpiece, ask yourself, What's the smallest unit of available genius?

What's the bar of music, the typed phrase, the personal human interaction that makes a difference?

Don't worry about changing the world. First, focus on making something worth sharing. How small can you make it and still do something you're proud of?

169. The Wild Side

In 1972, Herbie Flowers was a session musician. He showed up with his double bass guitar and did what was asked of him.

David Bowie had worked with Flowers on *Space Oddity*, so when Lou Reed asked Bowie for a recommendation, he made the connection to Flowers.

Reed gave Flowers a bar of music to play. In the moment, Herbie asked Lou if it was okay if he experimented a bit. He decided to do an overdub—using an electric bass to go ten notes above the double bass track he'd already recorded.

The result: the haunting backbone of "Take a Walk on the Wild Side." In twenty minutes, Herbie Flowers delivered a tiny bit of genius and ensured Lou Reed's career.

Of course, it took more than twenty minutes. It took a decade of building his craft and learning to see and to listen.

170. "How Do I Make This Better?" Is Different than "How Do I Make This?"

That's the way our culture works. It's easy to get a committee together to criticize the new logo that your agency put together. It's almost impossible to find someone willing to make the logo itself.

We're a community of critics and tweakers and tinkerers.

The reason is simple: it's safer. People rarely criticize the critic. And beyond that, it's not that hard to use sandpaper. It's a lot more difficult to use a bandsaw, or even to use a pencil to draw the plans in the first place.

There's a huge clue here about what to do next: *get a pencil*.

That's what's scarce. People who will draw up plans. People who will go first.

After that, you can easily get help from one of the people who are good at using sandpaper, now that you've done just about all of the scary bits.

171. Proving to Yourself that Creation Isn't Fatal

One of the reasons that anchor-up is essential is that you will start a cycle. You will alternate between success when you reach your anchor, and non-doom when you don't. Neither is fatal. This teaches us that promises won't lead to our destruction. We can make a sincere promise about the future if we believe we've got a shot at keeping that promise.

Overpromising is not a professional's habit.

Welcome to the practice.

And thus the idea of morning pages, of typing up everything that comes to mind, or the "yes, and" of improv. Each of these tactics is a way of persuading the other half of our brain that we're actually capable of doing this work on demand.

We promise to ship, we don't promise the result.

It doesn't matter if the work is good at first. How can it be? Was Richard Pryor hysterically funny the first time he went to an open mic night? Unlikely. Did Gödel revolutionize mathematics the first time he went to the chalkboard? Of course not.

What these first rounds of public work do is establish to the creator that it's survivable. Show up. Do your best. Learn from it.

And then we get to do it again.

172. What Does "Good" Mean?

No one wants to make lousy work. We seek out good or even great.

But how, exactly, do we judge our work? It might be a trap to ask someone else (or yourself) if your work is any good.

It's a trap because you might be tempted to judge "good" by commercial success. Or feedback from gatekeepers.

Was *Harry Potter* not good when it was rejected by twelve publishers? Did it suddenly become good after it became a worldwide phenomenon? How can the same book be good and not good at the same time?

Good needs to be defined before you begin. What's it for and who's it for? If it achieves its mission, then it's good. If it doesn't, then either you were unlucky, incorrect, or perhaps, what you created didn't match what you set out to do.

And yes, there's a huge gap between "good" and "as good as it could be." It's likely we'll never bridge that gap.

173. Protecting Your Perfect Idea

How much does it help you to know that you have something special in reserve, something unseen, something yet to be discovered?

You won't run out. This isn't your one and only shot. There's no perfect idea, just the next thing you haven't shipped yet.

No one is keeping you from posting your video.

No one is keeping you from blogging every day.

No one is keeping you from hanging your artwork.

The only way to get through the steps is to do the steps.

174. Alexander's Theorem of Professional Exceptionalism (and the corollary: the creative's failure narrative)

Ask a doctor or a therapist if they think they're above average for their profession. Odds are they'll tell you that they're not only above average, but that they're *well* above the average. Perhaps even in the top 10 percent.

Scott Alexander, writing on *Slate Star Codex*, identifies several reasons for this trend. Here are a few:

1. Therapists often get patients who have left another doctor. Therefore, the thinking goes, they must be better than that guy.

2. Patients are either cured (wow, I did a good job) or stop coming. The confident therapist either doesn't notice the attrition or chalks it up to a shift in insurance or

geography—or they were cured! Naysayers are invisible and silent.

3. Cognitive dissonance causes regular patients to be happy with their treatment—and they don't have anything else to compare it to, so the default is to believe that the experience is a great one.

The scarcity caused by professional accreditation plus the lack of clear comparative metrics means that all of these forces are amplified over the course of a career.

Compare this to the plight of the struggling creative. Call it the corollary of self-doubt.

For creatives, the opposite forces are often at work:

1. Because most of our work is purchased à la carte, and because there's far more supply than demand, most of the feedback we receive is rejection. Rejection comes not just from the market, but from self-confident gatekeepers who we perceive as knowing more than we do.

2. Because the work we do involves widely available tools (like a keyboard), the group of people who believe that they can also do the work (or improve on ours) is very large. No one knows everything at the very same time that everyone is an expert.

3. Because many of us have a transient base of fans (music lovers follow many musicians, not just one), there's a great deal of churn in the fan base. If someone stops producing, listeners simply shift. If your therapist retires, it's a crisis.

4. Because negative criticism is easier to spread than positive feedback, most public criticism of our work is negative. On the other hand, people who are fairly satisfied say nothing.

5. Because we work in novelty, our existing customers are often hesitant to return, because someone else (anyone else, actually) can offer more novelty than we can.

6. Because creative magic is truly breathtaking, the audience (and we) are chasing a once-in-a-lifetime moment. Those, by definition, are rare, and so most of our interactions don't meet that standard.

All of this is countered by the tribal effects of culture and the cognitive dissonance of fandom (combined in the new online phenomenon of "stans"), but this only affects a tiny percentage of working creatives.

And that's one more reason for the typical creative to doubt herself. The most commercially successful creators simply have two things that the rest don't: the benefit of the doubt plus tribal cognitive dissonance.

175. Genre, not Generic

The world is too busy to consider your completely original conception.

The people you bring your work to want to know what it rhymes with, what category it fits in, what they're supposed to compare it to.

Please put it in a container for us, they say. We call that container "genre."

That's not a cheap shortcut; it's a service to the person you're seeking to change.

Generic work is replaceable. A generic can of beans can come from any company, because they're all the same.

But genre permits us to be original. It gives us a framework to push against.

Shawn Coyne has written brilliantly about genre. Not generic, which is boring, but genre, which gives your audience a clue as to what this work is about.

What's the format? What should it cost? What does it remind me of?

Ski resorts are a genre. So are monster movies.

Without genre, we're unable to process the change you seek to make. It's too difficult to figure out what you are doing and for whom, so we walk away.

No one goes out of their way to get a copy of a commodity

because copies don't make change happen. Copies aren't worth much.

Genre is a box, a set of boundaries, something the creative person can leverage against. The limits of the genre are the place where you can do your idiosyncratic work.

To make change happen, the artist must bend one of those boundaries, one of those edges.

Generic is a trap, but genre is a lever.

176. Transformation Begins with Genre

Shawn Askinosie has changed the way millions of people grow, sell, and eat fine chocolate.

First, he began with a simple genre: "This is a chocolate bar." Then, as one of the pioneers of the artisanal bean-to-bar movement, he extended it to, "This is a handmade chocolate bar."

Over the last decade, Shawn and his daughter, Lawren, have grown his family chocolate company into a multimillion-dollar enterprise. But the company has a number of surprising rules and principles at work:

1. Direct trade: they personally meet every farmer who grows their beans.

2. Direct selling: they only sell directly to small companies that sell directly to the public.

3. Open-book management: everyone on his team is involved.

4. Persistent and generous community presence: they support their growers, as well as youth in their Missouri community.

It's worth noting, though, that there's no mistaking what he makes. Shawn's chocolate holds its own in worldwide competitions. His pricing is in the right ballpark for luxury chocolate in bean-to-bar. His packaging, customer relations, delivery systems—they all fit the genre.

Transformation begins with leverage. And you get leverage by beginning with genre.

177. How Is It Different?

What will I tell my friends?

Begin with genre. Understand it. Master it. Then *change* it.

Siegel and Shuster didn't invent comics, but they changed them with *Superman*. Warby Parker didn't invent eyeglasses, but the company changed the way people buy glasses by revolutionizing their supply chain. Lemontree didn't invent nonprofits that serve the poor, but they changed the approach and the metrics.

Before we can begin to make it different, we have to begin with what's the same.

Humans and chimps share almost all the same DNA. More than 98 percent is identical. What makes us not a chimp is the last little bit.

That's all you need.

The smallest viable breakthrough.

178. Back On the Hook

The hook is a reason to avoid genre.

We've been brainwashed into believing that artists with talent obey the muse and are vulnerable, personal, and without artifice. So what do they need a genre for? But more than that, because we realize that if we choose a genre, we've just made a series of promises.

If you tell us that this is a reggae record, we're going to compare you to Bob Marley. If you assert that you're painting fine art, you've got a thousand years of artists to stand next to.

It's so much easier to say, "It's just me." It's simply what I felt like creating.

Because then we'll ignore you.

And then you're off the hook.

179. Ernest Hemingway versus the Novel in Your Head

I've never met someone who didn't have a good idea somewhere inside.

Do you have one? Maybe more than one?

We all have a plan on how to make work better, or to change an organization we care about, or to fix some annoying broken thing in the world. Some of us have a poem, a song, or a novel rolling around as well.

What's the difference, then, between you and Gil Scott-Heron? He recorded more than twenty albums and revolutionized an art form.

It's not that Gil's songs are better than yours, or that Hemingway's writing is better than yours. It's that they shipped their work, and you hesitated.

Of course, at first, all work is lousy. At first, the work can't be any good—not for you and not for Hemingway.

But if you're the steam shovel that keeps working at it, bit by bit, you make progress, the work gets done, and more people are touched.

There's plenty of time to make it better later. Right now, your job is to make it.

180. Meetings Might Help, but They Probably Won't

As a company grows, the number of meetings grows even faster, eventually reaching a point where so many meetings are taking place that paralysis kicks in.

There are two reasons for this.

The first is simple math. More people needing to be in the loop means more meetings. But the math of more and more meetings clearly doesn't scale, which is why we invented memos, and eventually Slack.

No, the real reason is this: Meetings are a great place to hide. Meetings are where we go to wait for someone else to take responsibility. Meetings are a safe haven, a refuge from what might happen.

In every meeting, your work will interact with others. If you choose to go to meetings with people who are focused on expanding and amplifying your peculiar vision, then it's likely that your work will get better.

On the other hand, if you go to meetings with people who have an agenda around maintaining status roles, the status quo, and deniability, then the opposite is going to happen.

Over the last two decades, network TV executives held meetings where ideas went to die. At the same time, HBO, Netflix, and Showtime began to have meetings where showrunners were pushed to make their work more distinctive, not less.

Show me your calendar and tell me who you're listening to, and then we can discuss whether you have a similar problem.

181. A Roundup of Tips and Tricks for Creators

- Build streaks. Do the work every single day. Blog daily. Write daily. Ship daily. Show up daily. Find your streak and maintain it.

- Talk about your streaks to keep honest.

- Seek the smallest viable audience. Make it for someone, not everyone.

- Avoid shortcuts. Seek the most direct path instead.

- Find and embrace genre.

- Seek out desirable difficulty.

- Don't talk about your dreams with people who want to protect you from heartache.

Make Assertions

182. An Assertion Is Not a Guarantee

In December 2014, French musician Joël Roessel discovered something of monumental interest to vegans everywhere: you can take the water that's left in a can of chickpeas, called aquafaba, and turn it into foam . . . and then use it for whipped cream and other concoctions.

I wasn't in his kitchen when he figured this out, but I'm certain that before he was sure it was true, he asserted that it *might* be.

The liquid in cans of chickpeas has been around as long as there have been cans of chickpeas, but Roessel was the first person inquisitive enough to make an assertion like this one. Once made, the steps to test the assertion were pretty obvious.

"If I take this and do that to it, I'm asserting that something useful will come of it."

Assertions are the foundation of the design and creation process.

You can assert that a poem will help a teenager feel less lonely. You can assert that launching a conference on Ethereum will be useful and profitable. And you can assert that it might be worth asking a certain kind of music fan to listen to your new song.

183. Amanda Theodosia Jones and the Amplification of Voices

More than a hundred years before Roessel made an assertion about aquafaba and chickpeas, Amanda Jones invented and patented the process of canning fruit, which became a standard that is still in use around the world.

Jones turned her patents (she had more than any other woman of the 1800s) into the Women's Canning and Preserving Company, which was 100 percent owned and staffed by women. In the first three months, they shipped 24,000 orders.

The assertion that fruits could be canned without losing flavor was made years before she figured out how to do it. The brave act of building a significant women-owned and women-staffed company was put in place long before the orders arrived.

The practice demands assertions when there are no guarantees.

184. Egomania versus Ego Strength

We talk about ego like it's a bad thing.

Egomania is a bad thing. It's the narcissism that comes from only seeing yourself, from believing that you are immortal, invulnerable, and deserving of all good things that come your way. Or the feeling that all the art is for you and for you alone.

But ego?

Ego is required for us to find the guts to make an assertion.

What right do you have to speak up and offer to make things better?

What right to imagine that you have something to contribute?

What right to plow through the process, from helpless beginner to floundering mediocrity to working professional?

I think you have every right.

In fact, I think you have an obligation. That's why we share our planet with you.

Because we're counting on you to make an assertion and to contribute your work to make things better.

185. Assertions Are Not Answers and Assertions Are Generous

We've been pushed to have the answer. To know with certainty what's going to happen next. To be able to prove that we're right. To show our work.

And answers, in many settings, are essential. But answers end the conversation, either because your answer clearly solves the problem or because it doesn't. Answers don't begin the inquiry.

Assertions are the generous act of seeking to make things better. They're half a question. "Perhaps . . ." is the unstated word at the beginning of every assertion.

Before you find an answer, you'll need to make an assertion.

186. Buzzer Management

It's likely that you'll never be a contestant on *Jeopardy!*, but if you are, here's the secret to doing well:

You need to press the buzzer before you know the answer (but not before you realize that you have a process for getting to the answer).

Once you realize that you're the kind of person who can find the answer, once you know that you probably know the answer, buzz.

Then, by the time Alex calls on you, you'll have something to say.

Too often, we wait until we're sure we're right.

Better to begin with an assertion.

And then find out.

187. Intentional Action Requires Assertion

Intentional action isn't passive. It is a process of seeking to make a change happen.

And we can't squirm away from the gaze that comes with this. The way we acquire the attention and participation of others is by making an assertion.

Your assertion doesn't have to be for a large group. It doesn't have to be stated with certainty. But it has a function, and the function is to bridge the gulf between you and us, as well as the gulf between now and soon.

An assertion is a promise. A promise that you'll try. A promise that you'll ship. And a promise that if you fail, you'll let us know why.

188. An Assertion Is Generous

It involves making things better.

"I see the situation and I'm offering something to improve it."

Find your audience, then share a point of view and an invitation to connect around a new idea.

You can't design with intent unless you commit to who it's for and what it's for. And that leads to your assertion.

Often, we begin by simply making an assertion to ourselves. It might be too soon to invite the audience into our studio. But the act of claiming the assertion begins the cycle of better.

189. Demand Follow-Up Questions

An assertion is not a statement of authority. Managers have authority, so they don't need to make assertions; they simply make announcements.

But as a creative, you lead without authority. Instead, you rely on the wisdom of your insight and the desire you have to accept responsibility.

If you're going to accept responsibility, you want to be certain that people understand what you've just asserted.

Hence the follow-up questions.

What are the implications, ramifications, and side effects of what you plan to do? What are your contingency plans? What will happen if it works? (And if it doesn't?)

When you're leading people who are engaged in the work, the follow-up questions shouldn't be seen as skeptical or lacking in trust. In fact, it's the opposite. These are the questions of co-conspirators, of people enrolled to go on this journey with you.

If, "any questions," receives no response, you need to earn more enrollment and make your assertions more clearly.

190. It's a Conspiracy

The professional creative works to change the culture. Not all of the culture, certainly, but a pocket of it.

And culture is a conspiracy. It's the voluntary engagement of humans in search of connection and safety.

Your assertion begins a cultural shift, because it's an invitation for coconspirators to join you.

Andy Warhol traveled in a pack. Not just in a pack of other painters, but with musicians, filmmakers, and collectors. He didn't change the whole world, just part of it, and he began by challenging and changing his cohort.

Art and its magic can't happen in a vacuum. Even aided by the leverage of the internet, you're going to need others along for the journey. And your assertions, whether in word or in deed, are the way you begin that journey.

Organizing a conspiracy is fuel for your art.

Earn Your Skills

191. The Truth about Getting Better

Mundane doesn't mean what I thought it meant.

The word "mundane" actually refers to the real world: the practical, skills-based, reality-focused truth of the world around us.

In his breakthrough paper, "The Mundanity of Excellence," researcher Daniel Chambliss found the perfect laboratory to test for what it means to level up.

He reviewed the habits, backgrounds, and performances of competitive swimmers. It's an ideal population to examine because:

1. There are clear levels. From country-club league swimmers all the way up to the Olympics, participants are clearly in only one group in the hierarchy at a time.

2. Performance is easily measured. It's not like figure skating where the judges matter.

3. There are almost no external factors. The pool is the pool. Luck is easy to rule out, and performance can be measured over time.

4. There's a large and fairly varied population of competitors.

Here are the facts that he discovered:

There is no quantitative difference in training. People at higher levels of performance don't spend more hours training.

There is no requirement for social deviance. The athletes at the highest level had just as many friends and just as normal a life as dedicated swimmers at lower levels.

There is no talent differentiation. The ability to swim fast is not something you're born with.

In fact, there were two key differences between great competitors and good ones:

1. Skill. The best swimmers swim differently than the ones who don't perform as well. They do their strokes differently; they do their turns differently. These are learned and practiced skills.

2. Attitude. The best swimmers bring a different attitude to their training. They choose to find delight in the parts that other swimmers avoid.

This is their practice.

There isn't just one swimming culture, there are several. The swimmers who hang out at the country-club pool are very different in skill, approach, and affect than those who compete on the varsity team, and the culture of the varsity team isn't like the one among swimmers who compete at the Nationals.

It turns out that it's not training hours or DNA that changes outcomes. It's our belief in possibility and the support of the culture around us.

Creators have a better attitude, because they've figured out how to trust the process and trust themselves to work with it.

Attitudes, of course, are skills, which is good news for all of us, because it means that if we care enough, we can learn.

192. Look for the Cohort

The stories of amazing cultural institutions (Julliard, Black Mountain College, the Blue Note, The Actors Studio, etc.) imply that something secret and magical was taught or experienced inside of these hallowed buildings.

What probably happened was a cohort.

Cultural standards and normalization have enormous power over whether we choose a practice and how we find the guts to commit to our work.

Bob Dylan moved from Minnesota to Greenwich Village for a reason.

Most of the famous painters of the Renaissance came to Florence for a reason as well.

When you're surrounded by respected peers, it's more likely you'll do the work you set out to do.

And if you're not, consider finding some.

Find this cohort with intent. Don't wait for it to happen to you. You don't need to be picked—you can simply organize a cohort of fellow artists who will encourage themselves.

193. How Many Years Is Too Many?

Robert Caro, author of some of the most important biographies of the twentieth century, almost didn't finish his first magnum opus, *The Power Broker*. He had quit his job as a reporter, taken a modest advance, and moved his family to a tiny apartment. Year after year, he trudged through the book, writing more than a million words, but the end was never in sight.

In 1975, he wrote a poignant story for *The New York Times* describing his despair at the time. He knew no writers. He had little or no support from his friends, his publishers, anyone.

And then . . . he was given a key to a back room at the New York Public Library. Only eleven writers had keys, and each was given a desk at which to write.

He explains:

> Then one day, I looked up and James Flexner was standing over me. The expression on his face was

friendly, but after he had asked what I was writing about, the next question was the question I had come to dread: "How long have you been working on it?" This time, however, when I replied, "Five years," the response was not an incredulous stare.

"Oh," James Flexner said, "that's not so long. I've been working on my Washington for nine years."

I could have jumped up and kissed him, whiskers and all—as, the next day, I could have jumped up and kissed Joe Lash, big beard and all, when he asked me the same question, and, after hearing my answer, said in his quiet way, "*Eleanor and Franklin* took me seven years." In a couple of sentences, these two men—idols of mine—had wiped away five years of doubt.

Find your cohort. The generous ones.

194. None of Us Can Be Superman

Superman got boring. Every time Siegel and Shuster got him into a jam, or if the readers got bored, they added a new superpower.

X-ray vision, flight, time travel, orange kryptonite, heat vision— these were all added long after Clark was a kid in Smallville.

The problem with the model of the well-rounded superhero is

that there are very few well-rounded superheroes. It's much more likely that we'll succeed by overinvesting in just one or two skills. If we can do this without becoming a diva or sacrificing resilience, we have a chance to make a real contribution.

The challenge, then, is to have one superpower. All out of balance to the rest of your being. If, over time, you develop a few more, that's fine.

Begin with one.

195. Your Superpower Requires Commitment

Let's use organizations to help us understand what it means to commit.

You wouldn't hire FedEx to safely transport a fragile large item across the country. Their superpower is speed, not avoiding jostling. On the other hand, an art transport company might take a bit longer to get the vase to your new home, but their white-glove treatment (with actual white gloves) would make them an obvious alternative to FedEx.

"You can choose anyone and we're anyone" is not a useful way to earn customers, patrons, or supporters. Because if you're *anyone,* it's worth mentioning that a search engine is happy to point people to plenty of other people who are as *anyone* as you are.

In order to deliver speed at a low price, FedEx had to commit.

They made a significant number of choices all focused on that one metric. If you try to ship a very large (but very light) box via FedEx, you'll discover that instead of costing $30, it costs $450. That's because it breaks their system, and their system is their superpower.

When we think of an artist we admire, we're naming someone who stands for something. And to stand for something is to commit.

196. To Be Great Requires Embracing Neglect

Humans have even more trouble with superpowers than organizations do, because there's just one of you, and one of me. That means that if you're going to over-index for something, you're simply going to have to under-index for something else.

Fortunately, it's now possible to easily outsource many of the things you're not very good at, so that you can simulate a level of sanity and professionalism to the outside world.

But first, each of us must choose. Choose the skill we're going to assert to the outside world.

Even if it comes at the cost of neglecting some of the work you used to do that, in the end, was simply a distraction.

197. The Best in the World

In *The Dip*, I wrote about being the "best in the world." That doesn't mean that you're the best by every measure, nor does it mean that the world means the planet Earth.

To be the best in the world means that someone with options and information will choose you. Because your version of "best" matches what they seek, and because you're in their consideration set (their world).

It doesn't matter if there's a dermatologist in Tucson who has demonstrably better recovery rates for a certain sort of rash. You live in Iowa, and the bedside manner, reputation, and insurance policies of the doc down the street make her an obvious best choice for you. The tiny difference in measurable skill doesn't matter, not right here and right now.

Ultimately, the goal is to become the best in the world at being you. To bring useful idiosyncrasy to the people you seek to change, and to earn a reputation for what you do and how you do it. The peculiar version of you, your assertions, your art.

To announce and earn a superpower, one that's worth waiting for, seeking out, and yes, paying for.

You'll need to trust that this process makes it possible, and trust that you're the one to do it.

198. Earning a Skill

Traditionally, society assumed that artists, singers, artisans, writers, scientists, and alchemists would find their calling, then find a mentor, and then learn their craft. We can teach you to play scales, the thinking went, but we can't teach you to want to play. It was absurd to think that you'd take people off the street and teach them to do science or to sing, let alone persist at that teaching long enough for them to get excited about it.

Now that we've built an industrial solution to teaching in bulk, we've seduced ourselves into believing that the only thing that can be taught are easily measured "hard" skills.

We shouldn't be buying this.

We can teach people to make commitments, to overcome fear, to deal transparently, to initiate, and to plan a course of action.

We can teach people to desire lifelong learning, to express themselves, and to innovate.

And just as important, it's vital we acknowledge that we can *unteach* bravery and creativity and initiative. And that we have been doing just that for a long time.

Skills are more easily available than ever before. Not only the easily tested ones, but the real skills that drive our contributions and our reputation.

You can learn to learn.

199. Can You Teach Indian Food?

It's not easy to find young Anglo kids in Cleveland or Topeka who crave tandoori chicken or shrimp vindaloo. And yet kids with the same DNA in Mumbai eat the stuff every day. It's clearly not about genetics.

Perhaps households in Mumbai approach the issue of food the way school teaches a new topic. First, kids are taught the history of Indian food, then they are instructed to memorize a number of recipes, and then there are tests. At some point, the pedagogy leads to a love of the food.

Of course not.

People around the world eat what they eat because of community standards and the way culture is inculcated into what they do. Expectations matter a great deal. When you have no real choice but to grow up doing something or eating something or singing something, then you do it.

If culture is sufficient to establish what we eat, how we speak, and ten thousand other societal norms, why isn't it able to teach us a process to make art? Isn't it possible for the culture to normalize goal setting and passion and curiosity and the ability to persuade?

It can.

And you don't have to wait for it to happen. You can begin now.

200. Domain Knowledge: Did You Do the Reading?

It's absurd to go to a book group meeting and opine about a book you didn't read.

More absurd: Going to a PhD seminar and participating in the discussion without reading the material first. And, of course, no one wants to be operated on by a surgeon who hasn't read the latest journal articles on their particular procedure.

A first hurdle: Are you aware of what the reading (your reading) must include? What's on the list? The more professional your field, the more likely it is that people know what's on the list.

The reading isn't merely a book or journal, of course. The reading is what we call it when you do the difficult work of learning to think with the best, to stay caught up, to understand.

The reading exposes you to the state of the art. The reading helps you follow a through line of reasoning and agree, or even better, challenge it. The reading takes effort.

If you haven't done the reading, why expect to be treated as a professional?

A podcaster asked me a question, and I asked if he admired the path Krista Tippett had taken. He had no clue.

A colleague was explaining his work in memetics to me. I asked about Dawkins and Blackmore. You guessed it. He hadn't done the reading.

Or Kenji on food, Cader on publishing, Underhill on retail, Lewis on direct mail copywriting, and on and on . . .

You don't have to like their work or agree with their assertions. But you need to know who they are and what they're saying.

The line between an amateur and professional keeps blurring, but for me, the posture of understanding both the pioneers and the state of the art is essential.

Skill is earned.

201. Where Does Good Taste Come from?

Good taste is the ability to know what your audience or clients are going to want before they do.

Good taste comes from domain knowledge, combined with the guts and experience to know where to veer from what's expected.

Veer enough times, watch what the market does, and learn from that. That's the formula for good taste.

Good taste means that you understand genre and its benefits even more than the fans do.

It's worth noting that there isn't one market, there are many markets. If the people you seek to serve like what you think they're going to like, then you have good taste.

The shortcut, available to almost no one, is to simply create for yourself. If what you like and what the client likes are always in sync, you're in great shape . . . but almost always, over time, they drift apart, and so we end up with Liberace or Lou Reed. It's still creative work, but the clients fade away.

202. Knowing Is a Shortcut to Skill

Brian Koppelman, the renowned screenwriter and showrunner, has seen more movies than you have. He may have seen more movies than anyone I've ever met. And that's not merely a sign of passion. His understanding of what's come before gives him the platform and the standing to help figure out what's going to come next.

Growing up, I read every single book in the science fiction section of the Clearfield Public Library. From Asimov to Zelazny, all of them. Ten years later, when I launched a line of science fiction computer games, the domain knowledge opened the door to understanding what might work.

The point is not to copy, but in fact to avoid copying. Our best commercial work reminds people of what they've seen before.

Creativity doesn't repeat itself, but it rhymes.

203. In and of Itself

If you watch all forty-five episodes of *Monty Python's Flying Circus* playing simultaneously (you can: www.trustyourself.com/monty), what you'll immediately notice is that any given moment in any given episode is clearly Monty Python. The same thing is true for Star Wars movies and for Harry Potter books.

They are in and of themselves. The peculiarity is specific and consistent.

It's not duplicative or repetitive. But it rhymes. Just about every frame shows the fingerprints (and idiosyncrasy) of its creators.

We're under short-term pressure to remove all identifying marks. But in fact, the work that stands the test of time and finds its audience is filled with identifying marks.

It rhymes with itself.

Seek Out
Constraints

204. Constraints Create the Possibility of Art

It's tempting to rail against the boundaries. That you can't make a Kindle book as beautifully illustrated as you'd like, or electronic music as sophisticated as you're hoping to. There isn't enough time, there isn't enough bandwidth, or there isn't enough money.

But without constraints, we're left with no tension and no chance for innovation or surprise.

PS Audio makes some of the best stereo equipment in the world. And almost all of it is less than half the price of comparable products from competitors. That's because their products are engineered for assembly at scale and their components are chosen with cost in mind.

Without these constraints, they'd end up competing with a hundred other price-is-no-object niche designers, and it's unlikely that the added resources would lead to a notable improvement in their product.

By choosing their constraints, they are able to develop a

coherent approach to what to do next. The constraints are the foundation of their work.

All creative work has constraints, because all creativity is based on using existing constraints to find new solutions.

205. The Icon of Icons

Susan Kare was given 1,024 squares. That's it: 32 × 32, a simple grid.

Using graph paper and a pencil, she created the personality of the Mac, and based on her innovations, every computing device you've used over the last few decades. She built the first popular bitmap fonts, the tiny little folders, paint brushes, and smiling faces that we associate with using a smart device.

Someone might have seen the limits and whined about the lack of color or resolution. Susan, acting as a professional, saw the limits of 1,024 squares and smiled, because she knew that boundaries create a platform for important work.

206. Where Are the Mandolins?

R.E.M. was a solid indie band, but they'd never had a breakout pop hit. And after ten years on the road, they were in a rut and they knew it.

"I was a little bored with guitar," Peter Buck told *Rolling Stone*. "I had been playing it eight hours a day for all of my life."

When it was time for a new album, the band agreed to embrace a new set of constraints.

First, no touring: they did fewer than two dozen gigs the year they recorded *Out of Time*. The bassist switched to keyboards, the drummer switched to the bass, and guitarist Buck led with the mandolin, not the guitar.

"With Peter not wanting to play electric guitar, we started writing differently," one group member said. "The songs you write on an acoustic or a mandolin or balalaika or what have you, tend to be different than what you'd write on an electric guitar. We decided that we could write on different instruments rather than forcing ourselves to write different-sounding songs."

It would have been easy to lift the constraints, but the very tension the discomfort caused created the energy the band was looking for. And the record spent more than two years on the charts.

207. Wiggle Room

Would this book be better if it were longer?

The first instinct the generous creative may have is to ask for an extension. To insist on more colors, more leverage, more time.

To rail against the boundaries that fence us in, because if we just had a little more wiggle room, then we'd really be able to do something magical.

And so the network TV writer wishes she were on cable. And the cable TV showrunner believes it might be better if it were a movie. And the movie producer wants a development deal.

But . . . some of the most important work goes on in live theater, a room with no retakes, no special effects, and a tiny budget.

That's because it's constraints that enable us to create art.

Art solves problems in a novel way, and problems always have constraints.

208. You Can't Think Outside the Box

It's dark and cold outside the box.

But the edge of the box?

The edge of the box gives you leverage. When you find the edge of the box, you're in the place that has scared away those that came before you. It's from this edge that you can turn the constraint into an advantage, instead of an excuse.

209. Monty Python Found a Holy Grail

The original Monty Python TV show was hamstrung by constraints. It was short, it had a tiny budget, it had nothing but an ensemble cast, it was shot in black and white, and it had virtually no promotion. But, in fact, the very thing the show had going for it was the constraints.

Because expectations were so low, the cast and writers had very little oversight. Precisely because no one was expecting very much, they got away with quite a bit.

The same thing happened with their biggest hit movie. The budget was too small, the sets and costumes were laughable, and the ending appears to have been made up in the editing room.

And that's why the coconuts worked.

Have you ever noticed that big-budget comedies are almost never funny?

210. Susan Rothenberg Painted Horses

Almost always, horses. No fancy backgrounds, no highly polished marble, simply paintings of horses.

David Sedaris, Ken Burns, Oprah—each of them is a master of constraint. Each embraced a set, or a method, or a budget, and then inhabited that choice fully.

Consider that during its heyday, PBS TV had Julia Child, Mr. Rogers, Bob Ross, and *Sesame Street*. The budget for all four iconic shows wouldn't even pay for one show on a major network.

Finding the constraints and embracing them is a common thread in successful creative work.

211. Some Favorite Constraints

Time

Money

Format

Team members

User trust

Materials

Technology

Regulation

Physics

The status quo

You probably have no choice but to ease one or two of them. But the rest? They will persist and you can befriend them as you rely on them to amplify your creativity.

Constraints and your dance with them are part of the practice.

212. Change the World Doesn't Mean Change Everything

Bill Putnam changed recorded pop music by inventing reverb. In 1947, he put a microphone and a speaker in a bathroom and turned the song "Peg O' My Heart" into a No. 1 hit.

By daring to create artificial reverb, he opened the door for so much of what we hear coming from music studios today. He didn't do it to become famous (in fact, he didn't become famous). And he didn't do it to change everything. Instead, he did it because this little corner of this little industry was the place he chose to make a difference.

The change we seek to make can feel small indeed, but it all ripples.

One record, one interaction, one person . . . it might be enough.

213. Hubris Is the Dream Killer

The world is filled with overconfident people. Overconfidence leads to malpractice, to fraud, and to broken promises. Overconfidence is arrogance.

You don't want an overconfident surgeon or even an overconfident bus driver. By definition, overconfidence leads to risky behavior and inadequate preparation.

But the practice requires us to do our work without becoming attached to the outcome. It's not overconfidence, it's a practice of experiments that respect the pitfalls of hubris.

There's almost no downside to trusting yourself too much.

When we trust ourselves, we're focused on the process, not the outcome. The process of doing our work and paying attention to the outcome without requiring it to happen. The process of preparation and revision. And the process of caring enough to contribute.

Trusting yourself doesn't create overconfidence, because you're focused on the process, not on making promises you can't keep.

In fact, overconfidence is one of the symptoms that you might not trust yourself yet. Because overconfidence, like all forms of resistance, is a way to hide. Don't sabotage the work by ignoring the practice. Trust yourself to find a way forward, but seek out the resilience you'll need to persist as the practice continues.

214. Is the Moon Covered in Dust?

And if so, how deep is it?

When NASA set out to visit the moon and return safely, the dust theory was a raging controversy. Professor Thomas Gold of Cornell maintained that the surface was completely covered in fine dust, to an unknown depth. If the surface of the moon wasn't solid, it might be impossible to land or, even worse, to take off from the surface.

Overconfidence would have sent Apollo 11 to the moon without considering the possibility that the lunar lander would sink deep into the dust and the astronauts would never be able to return. A thoughtful, iterative process won out. We sent unmanned Ranger and Surveyor missions to the moon during the mid-1960s, partly to determine just how deep the dust was.

And to be safe, the Apollo 11 lunar module had 37-inch-wide landing pads on each leg—far wider than you'd use if you were sure of the density of the soil. The practice reflected an awareness of the risks and worked to reduce them.

The second thing Neil Armstrong said as he walked on the surface: "And the surface is fine and powdery. I can pick it up loosely with my toe."

Armstrong trusted himself and the process enough to do something legendary, but he never confused the practice of his mission with a guarantee that it was going to work perfectly.

215. Trust the Process

Trusting yourself doesn't require delusional self-confidence. Trusting yourself has little to do with the outcome.

Instead, we can learn to trust the process. This is at the heart of our practice. We can develop a point of view, learn to see more clearly, and then ship our work (and ship it again, and again). We don't do it to win, we do it to contribute. Because it's an act of generosity, not selfishness, we can do it for all the best reasons.

The practice is its own reward.

Trusting yourself comes from a desire to make a difference, to do something that matters.

Anyone who has ever learned to walk, talk, or ride a bike has gained these skills without full assurance that the effort would lead to success on any given day. But only the effort is under our control. The results are not.

By searching for (and then embracing) a practice that contributes to the people we care about, we can find a path forward. That path won't always work, but we can trust ourselves enough to stick with it, to lean into it, to learn to do it better.

The alternative is corrosive. When we begin to distrust our own commitment to the practice, we're left with nothing but fear. When we require outcomes as proof of our worth, we become brittle, unable to persist in the face of inevitable failure on our way to making a contribution.

No one can possibly do a better job of being you than you can. And the best version of you is the one who has committed to a way forward.

Your work is never going to be good enough (for everyone).

But it's already good enough (for someone).

Committing to a practice that makes our best better is all we can do.

216. Elements of the Practice

Creative is a choice.

Avoid certainty.

Pick yourself.

Results are a by-product.

Postpone gratification.

Seek joy.

Understand genre.

Embrace generosity.

Ship the work.

Learn from what you ship.

Avoid reassurance.

Dance with fear.

Be paranoid about mediocrity.

Learn new skills.

Create change.

See the world as it is.

Get better clients.

Be the boss of the process.

Trust your *self.*

Repeat.

217. You're Not the Boss, but You Are In Charge

You are in charge of how you spend your time. In charge of the questions you ask. In charge of the insight that you produce.

In the powerful, horizontal organization, each of us decides what to learn next, who to talk with next, and what to move up on the agenda.

This new freedom requires us to find a habit that will lead us to share our voices, even when it's inconvenient or frightening.

Without trust, we'll choose to hide out instead, letting the opportunity pass us by.

Mostly: you are in charge of the change you make in the world. Who else should be? Who else could be?

218. Tuesdays in the Anthropology Department

In 1983, Chip Conley changed my life.

I was one of the youngest students in my class at business school, and the first few weeks were pretty rough. One day, I found a small handwritten note in my mailbox. It was from Chip, who I didn't know. He invited me and a few other students with similar entrepreneurial backgrounds to form a brainstorming group every week.

He booked us a conference room in the anthropology department, a few buildings away. Why there? Because, he said, the only reason we'd ever be in this room is to have these sessions. We would come to associate the room with our process.

Over the next nine months, the five of us invented and outlined more than a thousand businesses. We backed into the practice because we weren't expecting an outcome. And it quickly became a habit to get into a peculiar state of mind, because, after all, that's what the room was for.

If you didn't want to be on this journey, don't be in this room.

Chip went on to become a bestselling author, teacher, and entrepreneur. But in that room, his career and mine actually got their start.

Because we decided to be in that room and to go on that journey.

219. Explore the Space

If you want more cowbell, it pays to listen to "fabled record producer" Bruce Dickinson. In the famous *SNL* skit, his character, portrayed by Christopher Walken, instructs the squabbling members of Blue Öyster Cult to "explore the space."

This confuses a lot of people. How can you explore the space without moving around? Why bother?

What Bruce is getting at is the idea of intentionally discovering the edges and corners of the work you've decided to do.

To go to one edge or another.

And then to go beyond the edge, because the only way to know it's an edge is to cross it.

As the artist George Ferrandi said, "If you have to ask 'should I keep going?' the answer is 'yes.'"

> *Life is on the wire,*
> *the rest is just waiting*
>
> PAPA WALLENDA[*]

Are you on the wire?

(Or are you just waiting?)

---

[*]Or possibly Matt Damon or Brian Koppelman and David Levien, depending on who you ask.

Where Do Ideas Come from?

Ideas rarely come from watching television.

Ideas sometimes come from listening to a lecture.

Ideas often come while reading a book.

Good ideas come from bad ideas, but only if there are enough of them.

Ideas hate conference rooms, particularly conference rooms where there is a history of criticism, personal attacks, or boredom.

Ideas occur when dissimilar universes collide.

Ideas often strive to meet expectations. If people expect them to appear, they do.

Ideas fear experts, but they adore beginners' minds. A little awareness is a good thing.

Ideas come in spurts, until you get frightened. Willie Nelson wrote three of his biggest hits in one week.

Ideas come from trouble.

Ideas come from our ego, and they do their best when they're generous and selfless.

Ideas come from nature.

Sometimes ideas come from fear but often they come from confidence.

Useful ideas come from being awake and alert enough to actually notice.

But sometimes ideas sneak in when we're asleep and too numb to be afraid.

Ideas come out of the corner of the eye, or in the shower, when we're not trying.

Mediocre ideas enjoy copying what happens to be working right this minute.

Bigger ideas leapfrog the mediocre ones.

Ideas don't need a passport, and often cross borders (of all kinds) with impunity.

An idea must come from somewhere, because if it merely stays where it is and doesn't join us here, it's hidden. And hidden ideas don't ship, have no influence, and make no intersection with the market. They die, alone.

If You Had Tomorrow to Do Over Again, Would You?

Better is possible. But not if we continue to settle, continue to hide, and continue to scurry along the same paths.

We have more to do.

We need your contribution. But it can't happen and won't happen if we can't figure out how to trust ourselves enough to do the work.

Unquenchable

You made it to the beginning.

What happens now?

For a very long time, people have been telling you that you didn't have the right paperwork, weren't chosen, weren't good enough.

And now, perhaps, you see that it's all been up to you. In fact, it's up to each of us.

Where is the fuel to keep us going?

Anger gets you only so far, and then it destroys you. Jealousy might get you started, but it will fade. Greed seems like a good idea until you discover that it eliminates all of your joy.

The path forward is about curiosity, generosity, and connection. These are the three foundations of art. Art is a tool that gives us the ability to make things better and to create something new on behalf of those who will use it to create the next thing.

Human connection is exponential: it scales as we create it, weaving together culture and possibility where none used to exist.

You have everything you need to make magic. You always have.

Go make a ruckus.

The magic is that there is no magic.

Start where you are.

Don't stop.

Acknowledgments

This book was inspired by you—anyone who has cared enough to lean into the work and make things better.

My five conversations on *The Moment* with Brian Koppelman (along with my close listening to his one hundred best interviews) had a huge impact on how I think about the ideas in this book. He cares about where the magic comes from.

The writing, friendship, and support of Margo Aaron, Gabe Anderson, and Eliot Peper have been priceless. I hope you get a chance to read all three of them. And of course, Steven Pressfield, reluctant father of Resistance.

Patricia Barber, Cyrille Aimée, Christian McBride, Sarah Jones, Jodi Spangler, Susan Kare, Peter Gabriel, Rosanne Cash, Simon Sinek, Will Guidara, Christina Tosi, Ann Marie Scichili and so many others talked with me, modeled the behavior, and generously held the door open for so many who followed.

Thanks to Helene, Alex, and Mo who read early drafts, and for everything else (of course). And especially thanks to Niki Papadopoulos, who brings magic, and Adrian Zackheim, who raises the bar. Thanks to Tami Simon, Liz Gilbert, Pema Chödrön, Zig Ziglar, Lewis Hyde, Kevin Kelly, Patti Smith, Paul Jun, Roz and Ben Zander, Susan Piver, Jim Ziolkowski, Anthony Iannarino, Shawn Askinosie, Nancy Lublin, Pam Slim, Tobi Lütke, Fiona McKean, Harley and Lindsay Finkelstein, Liz Jackson, Scott Page, Bob Dorf, Tom Peters, Sarah Kay, Amy Koppelman, Danny Meyer, Nicole Walters and so many others who have changed the way I think and who might find their ideas in this book. And thanks to John Acker and Beena Kamlani for professional and generous work on deadline and at least one semicolon. And thanks to Kimberly Meilun for her gracious and unflappable manuscript wrangling.

I'm grateful to the Akimbo team, including Alex, Sam, Marie, Taylor, Grayden, Ishita, Meg, Czar, Avraham, Dean, Kristin, Scott, Louise, Pete, Travis, Francoise, Imogen, Colin, Jaime, and so many of our other coaches and students.

Bernadette Jiwa and Alex DiPalma have been role models, coconspirators, and ruckus makers. It's a privilege to know them.

ACKNOWLEDGMENTS

Thanks to Anne Shepherd for twenty years and twenty books and all the rest. It's hard to imagine this journey without your consistent and unflagging support. I've never dedicated a book to you before, and it's a privilege to do so right now.

And thanks to the many people who were part of the first session of *The Creative's Workshop*. You contributed more than five-hundred thousand actionable ideas to one another, all in service of shipping the work.